PRAISE FOR KEKI N. DARUWALLA

'It [*For Pepper and Christ*] is rich, generous and poetic … the bustling of souk and street, of the Red Sea ports and the wharves of Sidon, is conjured so vividly one can smell the incense and taste the salt … Elsewhere it opens out, the sea swells and glitters, maps are talked of rhapsodically and there is a tremendous sense of history blowing on its unstoppable way. Daruwalla moves surely from the grand prospect to the detail, from brutality to tenderness, and the book, as it becomes darker, is still shot through with dazzling colour' —**Anita Mason on *For Pepper and Christ, The Warwick Review***

'*For Pepper and Christ* is indeed an unusual and exceptional first novel' —**Gillian Wright, *India Today***

'The Cairo of the time reminds us of one of the novels of Nobel Laureate Naguib Mahfouz … Daruwalla's research is formidable. Each character rings true and captures the moods of the fifteenth century splendidly' —**K. Natwar Singh on *For Pepper and Christ***

'He [Daruwalla] has a desperately independent air, as if he was born full-grown from the head of some hitherto unrecognized goddess of poetry … *Under Orion* is impressive evidence not only of mature poetic talent but of literary stamina, intellectual strength of mind and social awareness' —**Nissim Ezekiel**

'The tension of cynical, skeptical modern outlook given shape through a tightly controlled, somewhat conservative technique makes Daruwalla's verse unique, like a compact but open metal structure, held together by its bolts and joints, filled with stresses waiting to explode' —**Bruce King**

'… both tough and gentle, virile and receptive. It shows that a man need not be afraid of the woman in him after all and that, yes, verse that is sophisticated need not take away from its power' —**Adil Jussawala on *A Summer of Tigers***

'Daruwalla has, from his very first book tended to let the atoms fall here one day and there the next, as Virginia Woolf said about life itself' **—Eunice D'Souza**

'Few Indian English poets have done with, or for, their language, what Keki N. Daruwalla has done ... We have here an alert intelligence, a barometer of the severe pressures exerted upon an individual by a predatory culture' **—Ranjit Hoskote**

'Daruwalla has been a force in Indian poetry for far longer than many up and coming novelists in India ... Forget watching *What Lies Beneath* and *Gladiator*, this is a better way to spend three hours' **—Nilanjana S. Roy on *Night River***

'There are poets like W.B. Yeats who keep reinventing themselves all their lives. Their sweep is vast, output prolific since they experiment with diverse forms of poetic expression. Keki Daruwalla belongs to such an illustrious lineage' **—M.S. Nagarajan, Literary Review, *The Hindu***

'There is sheer artistry in character portrayals. The nuances of Indian life in different social stratas have been ably presented and the style promises a new ethos in English writing in India' **—A.K. Dutta on *Sword and Abyss, India Today***

'Daruwalla loads every rift of his stories with the ore of experience. It is not simply that he has travelled and thought much, it is the experience of writing that gives his stories their weight and paradoxically, their delicacy' **—Shobhana Bhattacharji, *The Book Review***

'Daruwalla's fiction displays an impeccable command over fact and detail. Both engrossing and memorable, it certainly makes for very good reading' **—Makarand Paranjape**

'... one of India's most gifted short story writers' **—Anushree Majumdar, *Indian Express***

'Keki N. Daruwalla is indeed one of the most accomplished poets in India' ***—The Pioneer***

SWERVING TO SOLITUDE

LETTERS TO MAMA

Keki N. Daruwalla

SIMON &
SCHUSTER

London · New York · Sydney · Toronto · New Delhi

A CBS COMPANY

First published in India by Simon & Schuster India, 2018
A CBS company

1 3 5 7 9 10 8 6 4 2

Simon & Schuster India
818, Indraprakash Building,
21, Barakhamba Road,
New Delhi 110001

www.simonandschuster.co.in

Hardback ISBN: 9789386797223
eBook ISBN: 9789386797230

Typeset in India by SÜRYA, New Delhi

Printed and bound in India by Replika Press Pvt. Ltd.

FSC www.fsc.org MIX Paper from responsible sources FSC® C016779

Simon & Schuster India is committed to sourcing paper that is made from wood grown in sustainable forests and support the Forest Stewardship Council, the leading international forest certification organisation. Our books displaying the FSC logo are printed on FSC certified paper.

Contents

Coming Home

Sometimes you get down at the wrong station. You find it is also the wrong night, or worse, wrong dream. It happens when time has not got its screws fixed right. Time never got a mechanical engineering degree from a reputed college. Our auto mechanics do a better job as they steal hub caps, rear view mirrors or the car itself. They are good at screwing. So are lawyers, but that's another world, law courts I mean—a metaphor in miasmal mist—how I love my alliterations, Mama. Law courts mean the surreal suspension of belief. How's that for a definition?

You need to be careful when you are tired, and I sure was. I had enjoyed it for a while, as we set out close to dusk. We moved out of the station's steel trappings and the foothills fanned out, while trees and pylons slipped by. Failing twilight slowly chiselled away at the shrinking landscape. When it got dark I watched the lighted geometries of our glass windows spill across the tracks and race back to nowhere. Yes, I was returning home, but things change; time is the culprit again, it changes without notice. The damp on the window glass didn't let me see much. As the night train grated to a halt I found myself disoriented. If you shout 'where am I?' guys will look at you in an odd manner. You sense you are in some sort of trouble. I did. Damp on the window pane prevented me from seeing where I was, told you that. The dream didn't let me see beyond the eyelids. I seemed to have been everywhere, it had been something like a rim-of-the-earth *parikrama* down there, I mean between me and the closed eyelids. When I got down I had been fighting brush and bramble every yard in my hazy half-dream. Now it was concrete reality, I was in a maelstrom of torsos and elbows. I called out to the porters 'jaldi aao, trolley lao!'—there was no one there, I mean porters; trolleys in their rust red there were in plenty, lying abandoned. I could have shouted 'coolie' but that would upset me for the night. Coolies went to the Caribbean, didn't they? There were no shoulders on offer you could unload your baggage on.

The steps leading to the over-bridge were not a party, the whole world seemed to be there climbing to nowhere. You lug your bags, your kurta sticking to your back like a second skin. The monsoon rains are here. Sand doesn't lash Charbagh anymore. The night moths hover around the platform lights—Urdu poets make a big deal out of *shama* and *parwana*, flame and moth, the male dying at the touch of his beloved's beauty. (Let the bugger get his hands on her and within five years of wedlock he'll go for a mistress while she is having her third baby. So much for poetry, not forgetting love.)

The hills were better—I understood the language of the wind in the poplars. I knew a Himalayan thrush the moment I spotted its blue in the shrub. The night sky was sharper there. Star-clusters spoke to you—Orion, Taurus the bull with its horn, and of course the Great Bear, the only constellations I can read. Isn't it a shame, you live over two decades in this universe and all you know in the skies are three constellations! But I am here. Lucknow is another language. I spot an *ekka*, *tonga*, *tum-tum*—call it what you will, our one horse carriage, the driver clicking his tongue to encourage the horse. There are no cycle rickshaws to be seen. Where is everybody? What has happened to this bloody place? I notice that the tonga driver has a skull cap and a mixed black and white beard. Now if he can only agree at this hour. 'Qaiserbagh,' I shout, as I struggle with four other passengers, all equally desperate. Crowds and desperation are twin brothers, I feel. Too many people in the country, we want less bums, torsos, legs—sterilize the fellows! But philosophy has to take a back seat, you wanna get home.

'Fifty bucks!' I shout, flashing the first notes I can scrape out of my purse. He lets me in, telling the others respectfully to wait, doesn't elbow them out. Vanishing dregs of Lakhnavi tehzeeb. 'You don't have to give me all that,' he says. When I get down at home he accepts only thirty-five, and waits till I get my key into the lock—always tricky business at night, the streetlight across the road has turned iridescent in the haze. I struggle and manage (that's the story of my life)to open the house. Locks click open now and then, though spaces don't. I am home.

At night I noticed that trains and the sound of trains ran through my mind on parallel tracks. One dream, two tracks.

Letters to Mama

Of course, these will never be inserted in a mail box. I don't like the imperial red. We haven't been able to change the colour. That would need imagination and where are we going to get the wretched thing, imagination I mean? A bit puzzling, this. We day dream a lot—not many can beat us Indians when it comes to that—eyelids open and the future drooling away. My friends at college—Isabela Thoburn, if you please—dreamt of pimple-scars vanishing from their not exactly beautiful faces. Some girls dreamt of long tresses they were not blessed with and some dreamt of the Bombay film world, which was a snare for dreams. The soldier in his LOC dugout dreams of peace, and IIT-types dream of MIT or placements, I suppose. Judges, of course, dream of vacations, never mind the thousand-odd cases on each dusty table, paper and exhibit turning brittle, mouldering away on shelves, blood-stained knives getting rusted at the edges, under-trials gathering layers of fungus in jails. The shopkeeper dreams of money. His short-changed wife (the *bahu* didn't bring enough dowry) dreams of an auspicious moment when she could set her alight. Kerosene and match are such a matchless combination, I am happy with the pun, if that's what it is, Mama.

There are other reasons why these letters will not be posted: you don't write to the dead.

Well, life hasn't been a walk along the Gomati exactly since you left. But you would've approved of what I did. It was as ordinary a morning as any, the paper got dropped at my door, milkman on bicycle, his cans clanging away, woke me up with his cycle bell. How the hell did he know I was back? Intuition, I suppose. I would be lying if I said I heard the cucumber seller shouting away in the time-honoured Lakhnavi style:'*Laila ki ungliyan, Majnoon ki pasliyan khaye laio, khaye laio, khaye laio.*' Cucumbers tender as Laila's fingers and Majnoon's ribs, eat them, eat them, eat them.

I noticed the level light of Lucknow as I stepped out. I walked out into the street, nondescript like most other bloody streets—I am using the blood word pretty freely now that you are gone and there's no one to check me, Mama. But I will try not to use the F-word, since you hate it. Promise!And please note I think of you in the present tense.You will always be with me, and I am not being senty…I mean sentimental, if you didn't get that. A street like any other, haberdasheries, hardware shops, betel kiosks, tea boiling away in lidless pans, blackened on the insides by tannic acid, the outer bit by coal fires; and lest I forget, cows foraging in dirty municipal garbage bins. I noticed rickshaws stood almost in the middle of the road, while a car looped its sinuous way around them. Yes, and I saw the police sealing a hardware shop.

Two constables held lac (perhaps a short form of laquer?) sticks over a burning candle, and as those sticks started dripping, an iron seal was jammed into the gluey melt and later stamped on the cloth-bound lock. It took some time, for the candle wick was snuffed out twice by the breeze, till the Sub-inspector made one of the wide-buttocked constables stand downwind and shield the flame. Never were a cop's buttocks put to better use.

The shutters were down in any case, and the owner had placed his own lock there. They could have sealed the owner's lock, couldn't they? This hardware shop sold wash basins, kitchen sinks made of steel, shower stands, flush toilets. I had seen the swanky insides some years back. There was an ironmonger nearby, a small shop selling nuts (which Father Time had forgotten to screw properly, remember?), bolts, hammers, hacksaws, even utensils, *degchi*s and scrap iron plentiful as cow dung in a cattle pen. One time, a snake was discovered in the scrap iron. This shop was untouched. How could the hardware guy have offended the law, sorry state, for there was no law. Laws and legal codes, penal and procedural, had been sucked into Mrs Gandhi's dark pit of paranoia. And they were sealed the way the rusty shutters with the rusted Godrej lock were. The Supreme Court on Hardinge Road, recently named after Tilak, had itself sealed the Fundamental Rights in its judgement. Sometimes I become brave without being conscious of it, without any blood racing through my veins.

'Sir, why are you sealing this shop?'

He looked me up and down from my Kolhapuri chappals, bandaged big toe and silver *payal* right up to the remnants of *sindoor* in the parting on my head.

'Hmmm.'

'Is that supposed to be an answer?'

'The wise understand a word, a cough, a snort. For fools even the Ramayana won't suffice.'

This Sub-inspector had missed his vocation for sure; he should have been scribbling dialogues for Bombay films. Javed and Salim would have been out of business. Meanwhile another cop appeared on the scene, who seemed to oversee the order in the street. (You will notice Mama, that I refrained from saying 'law and order.' If you have a stick, there is order in the streets. Why must the state be loaded with law?) He never touched the lock or the shutters—didn't want to soil his hands. Had to be a senior guy. I asked him the same question. He countered with another—again, a sign of seniority. Are you a journalist?

'No Sir, just a member of the public.' Mama, you know, one has to lie sometimes. Anyway I was a castaway journalist at the moment, writing on hills and Kangra paintings, instead of the rumbustious, roistering reality (one could die for such an alliteration, Mama) we were confronted with.

'*Han*, and of course it is your right to know why a shop is being sealed, though I thought that there has been some rearrangement (*rad-o-badal*) in this business of rights since Madam's Emergency announcement.'

I nodded. It was wise to nod during this emergency. 'You must be having your reasons, Inspector Sahib.'

'For?'

'For sealing that shop.'

'We have nothing to do with reason, lady. We work under orders. Some iron bars and bolts are locked up, how it matter? Tell me how it matter? We are not handcuffing someone. Orders need to be obeyed, understand, even by girls of twenty.'

'Twenty-five.'

He wasn't happy being corrected—another sign of seniority.

'I asked about the sealing, Sir.' He didn't seem to register my polite reminder and just stared at the wall behind me, an off-white wall with a wet yellow streak—someone had obviously pissed on it minutes ago, pyjama dragged down to knee length, the cord held in one hand, a surreptitious look right and left and you let go.The bladder blesses you. That's just imagination Mama, I didn't see him piddling, just an encomium to the male bladder. 'Sealing that shop with its shutters down and locked by the owner in any case, solid Godrej lock? You still needed to seal it with lac.'

'Well said [*theek boli*]. You have heard of the house of lac, *Bitya*? Or did your parents forget to teach you the Mahabharata?'

'They forgot, but my boyfriend did not [wanted to shock him]. He told me about the Pandavas and the House of Lac, rather Lakshagraka, erected in days by Purochana in the forest of Varnavat.The Pandavas entered the forest on the eighth day of Phalguna. But they had got a dark hint that things were dicey here, and when the palace was set ablaze they were not there. Absence of body—key safety measure in a fire—ask any fireman.You can't burn absence, Inspector Sahib. It is all there in the Adi Parva 114 of Mahabharata, Sir.'

He nodded approvingly, but his look disapproved. Senior people don't like upstarts to know more than them, and be bold enough to spit it out.

'But there is this iron monger right here, dirty little shop stuffed with scrap iron, some of it rusted.How come you are not sealing it? No orders,I suppose.'

He didn't nod or bother to reply. People had gathered around this chit of a girl asking the police questions. My trouble is I look far younger than I am. Must be related to someone big, they may have thought.And these coincidences zap me, for just as I thought this up, the senior cop turned to the junior and said,'*Bade baap ki beti hogi*'.

A police truck rolled in and men clambered down.

Policemen create a lot of noise coming down a truck, right till the moment their hob-nailed boots thud against the tarmac. I could now feel the fear in the air. Fear communicates without sound, smell or any of the things we associate with the senses. The seventh sense, what? And fear is a communicable disease. But it turned to panic the moment they saw two hospital vans screaming to a halt. Police was *tamasha*—you watched them as you'd pause to watch bears dancing to a *damru*. But the hospital vans they knew would go for their privates—sorry Mama, but those are the facts.

These days, our days, one apologizes for facts. If facts had faces they would be embarrassed.

Pandemonium, Mama. The Pandies (alliteration led me on to that word) never ran from the avenging Brits as the rickshaw crowd ran. Remember the forced march of the Brits from Allahabad to Kanpur, as they went about stringing up mutineers on roadside trees. 1857 Mama, you knew the subject. (You were an expert on the Kakori conspiracy too, Mama. Your daughter is only an expert on kakori kababs.) To continue the narrative, as academics would put it, I have only read about grapeshot, but the humans flying away on all sides were as close to that as possible. How they scampered, leaving rickshaw, pushcart and tonga behind.

(You weren't offended by the term Pandies, were you Mama? I am irritated with all this drummed up rhetoric about freedom-fighters. The term has lost its sheen after all the money some of them made. And some of them are siding with Mrs Gandhi during the Emergency. Hence 'Pandies' out of cussedness.)

There were shouts of vasectomywalahs, *nasbandiwaleh*! That was it! Stupid me, I realized now why there were no porters and rickshaw-pullers at the station. They had bolted. The street was now seething with policemen, they were all over, not really brandishing their staves for once. They were hollering all right, though. They had been tutored to placate the guys if you please. 'Nothing is gonna happen to you son. Just relax and come with us into those mobile vans. You'll get *jalebi*s for free.' Doctors were also soliciting…will you lie down on my table/ said the doctor to the guy/ I'll use the most harmless scalpel/ your tool did ever spy. They made kissing sounds, *puchkarna* as we say in Hindi. Onomatopoeic. Sad isn't it, that language should have evolved from sounds emanating from kissing and necking, or hitting a fellow—or how else could a word like 'thud' have come into being? (Am not talking of Thadanis, Mama). Suddenly, I heard a man saying, 'like any other'. Where had he sprung from? How did I not notice him earlier? Did he sidle up to me? He saw the question in my eyes as I turned my head, and nodded. 'Like any other', he repeated.

'You seen many of these?' It was more a statement than a question. He just nodded. He sported a two-day stubble, wore the regulation jeans—you can't be a reporter if you're not in jeans. Five feet ten, I surmised, face burnt by the sun. Had to be a reporter.

'And you?'

'My first one.'

'Where the hell have you been? Timbuctoo?'

Rude bastard. 'Kangra.'

'Got a pad up there?'

Why was he asking? Wanted to shack up with me or what? 'Sort of.'

He nodded again; nodding seemed to come naturally to

him. '*Bade baap ki beti*.' He was still nodding to himself, as he said that aloud, more to himself than me. When a foreigner breaks into Hindustani, it rattles me, Mama. I don't know why. Just the surprise sprung on unsuspecting me, verbal bloody ambush. And I had heard the wretched words for the second time within minutes.

'Not really. Communist *ma ki ladki*.'

His incessant nodding was getting on my nerves. '*Communist ma ki bourgeois beti*,' he said, as if confirming a report he had already got from one of his sources.

'Wish I had a camera.'

'Lucky you. If you had one they'd have smashed it, and taken you in.' Then he looked me over, head to bruised toe. 'I saw you asking questions off the inspector, and surmised you were a journalist. But you seem to be an utter novice. Chummy with your editor or what? How come he hasn't fired you?'

'I thought you had brains. We are not allowed to write—unlike you guys who still manage to worm your way into your native press.' I was happy with that native bit. He laughed and extended his hand. 'Hemming.'

He doesn't hem and haw, I thought; didn't hide his identity. Thought he'd say I am John or Smith or something. 'They must have given you a first name, or did your parents forget?'

'They didn't,' he answered. 'Alfred.' He again extended his hand and this time I shook it vigorously. 'Welcome to Lucknow, Alfie.'

'You know why they have sealed that shop? He is a Jana Sangh guy. Very staunch. When young, he used to go to the *shakhas*.'

'You mean the khaki knickers and the solar- plexus-salute types?'

'You never been to a shakha, have you? I can see it in your eyes. Amazed how your editor hasn't booted you out!'

For a foreign correspondent he seemed to know quite a bit. They don't get their pounds for nothing. The more Alfie seemed to know, the more I hated him, and so my rudeness matched his. 'Which rag do you work for?' Before he could answer the older cop summoned me with his forefinger, the way you summon a hotel waiter. 'Dangerous man,' he muttered under his breath. 'Keep away from him.' For a moment I was too angry to even speak. What does one say at such a moment?

By now the acting rights had passed on to the victims. They too had a part in the play—they always have, there would be no play if there weren't victims, no scandals or enquiry commissions if there weren't any fall guys. The street detritus and the cops were at it, not just the cops but also the hospital staff. No vasectomy, no pay, that was the rule, a fiat handed down by the health minister. (I'll write a novel one day Mama, showing the minister of health down with syphilis and the finance minister fighting bankruptcy proceedings. Personal bankruptcy Mama, wouldn't want the country to go bankrupt.)

The street turned into a battle scene, more an end-of-battle scene, with street vendor and rickshaw-puller suddenly trying to break loose. Two of them had darted from a mobile van, one of them naked—I mean sans pyjamas or undies. That's how we define nudity, don't we? You can cover your torso with a trench coat, but the privates are the things wherein you'll catch the conscience of the king. But then there's something rotten in the state of Denmark at the moment, isn't it? Sorry I keep getting off the track, but as I said it was an end-of-the-battle scene, with cops in khaki and compounder and ward boy in white overalls, even a doctor with his gloves on, giving frantic chase. I can't say who was more frantic, the emasculators or the about-to-be emasculated?

So far the cops were only brandishing their sticks, herding the runaways, as goatherds nudge their flock back into the sheepfolds at dusk. But when a guy hit one of the victims, I couldn't restrain myself. I ran towards the fellow, never mind my hurt toe and slapped him full on the face. Can you imagine the humiliation for a Kanaujia constable, why he could even be from Bihar, getting slapped by a pheemale! Can one even contemplate the indignity of it? Mama, I leave the rest to your imaginasun. After all you have Bihari blood in you, what if you studied in the Loreto convent in Lucknow. Your mother was from Bihar. But to continue with the narrative from which I continually get derailed, the young sub-inspector, the dialoguewalah, the one who should have been writing speeches for Pran or some other villain, pounced on me and tried to pin my arms down, but I freed my right hand and threatened to slap him. The dialogue was fit for a film, he didn't have to invent it:

Sub-inspector (pouncing): 'How dare you slap a Policeman!'

Me: 'How dare you cut off their *lulus*!'

Doctor (bouncing in): 'We're not cutting them off. This is false propaganda.'

Me: 'Three cheers for the Emergency. Indira Gandhi ki jai!'

The sarcasm should have been evident, but they were taken aback. That cheer from me fell like a grenade. Guys didn't know what to do. What do you do to a mad girl who first slaps you and then raises a cheer for Mrs Gandhi! But khaki can't freeze for ever. The senior man, the inspector, sauntered towards where I stood and I saw him nod his head and say something—all I caught was the tail end of a short sentence… 'no handcuffs'. Two policemen stood on each side, holding me firmly by the wrists. When I struggled, the inspector gave me a kind look but shook his head from side to side. My resistance subsided momentarily. I reckoned it would be the cooler.

❁

The police call it embussing, Mama. So does the army. Ever heard the term? So we were put in a bus, taken to a police station and sent off to jail, where we de-bussed! I had heard the senior cop telling the SI to take me to the police station and not the control room. It was in jail I learnt that the control room had got very fierce pro-Emergency officers, loyalists of whom Sanjay Gandhi would have been proud, had he heard of them. But news of loyal riff raff never reaches royal riff raff. I was told the old man had done me a good turn. The control room would have booked me under Section 216, coming in the way of a public servant and his duty. Why don't we do away with this sham and start calling the police and the IAS types 'public overlords' and not servants?

Not that I didn't create a ruckus even in jail. A warder had to fill in the particulars of the new arrivals. 'Father's name?' he asked in a slow drawl—the man was unshaven and pot-bellied. 'Dead,' I answered. He did not lose his composure. Equanimity and fat bellies, I was to discover, are at peace with each other. 'Mother's name?' He asked. 'Dead,' I answered again.

'We are looking for names, not whether they are alive

or dead.' The fellow missed his chance of a good riposte. I reflected later that had I been him (God forbid) I'd have said, 'This ain't a headcount in a graveyard, Lady.'

Then the jailor appeared, looked at me carefully and said 'keep her in solitary.' I protested.

'It will be better for you if you stay there,' he said softly. And when I protested further he made me walk past the women cells. They stared at me wide-eyed in almost shocked silence. What could they be thinking of? Has the girl murdered someone, her boyfriend perhaps? The next cell contained prostitutes—victims of a massive raid. After all, sexual liberty also had to be contained, isn't it? Or what would Delhi say? The wireless message from the IG police to the home minister must have read 'so many prostitutes arrested'. The home minister must have banged his head on the table and screamed 'we want politicians arrested!!!' To get back, the women yelled at me and some of them stretched out their arms through the bars to get at me. I agreed with the jailor. It was solitary for me for two nights.

I was let off by evening after signing a bond which said I would keep the peace. My day for moving out of stereotypes. Compassionate jailor! What did he see in me to be kind?

Dr Bajpai came over to look at my big toe, if you please. She must be in her mid-sixties, Mama. Her glasses have become thicker since I last saw her. It felt as if I was looking at someone on the other side of a window. Shut window obviously, disapproval seemed to have been shut or shuttered there. For good. Shilpa had told her about it, my toe. Shilpa must have also tattled or how did she know I had been in jail. It wasn't in the papers. It was the two nights there that worried her. Wonder what she must have imagined—some fat scruffy looking jailor making advances? Who can tell? I was, of course, worried about what my husband in Delhi would do once he came to know.

'I don't know what your mother would have said, if she had learnt about it, slapping a policeman and a night in jail!'

'I wrote to her about it.'

You should have seen her face Mama, your doctor friend's. Shock sat on those ever pale cheeks as if it had a long lease there. She didn't pursue the matter, may have noticed my one millimetre smile. She couldn't have read anything in my eyes, for I determinedly looked serious. She felt unsure though, has this girl gone bonkers? She handed over antibiotic pills, and said she'd send over her compounder to bandage my toe.

'Seema, your big toe is infected, don't wear chappals for the next few days, or it could get worse, with the dirt. Put on shoes. You might as well stay home. You could keep out of trouble that way.'

Nice parting shot and a cold stare to go with it. On her way out she repeated, 'I'll send the compounder to bandage your toe.'

'That won't be necessary, Aunty. I will manage that.' It was Shilpa. If Dr Bajpai was here, could Shilpa be far behind? Not after she had tattled. Who else could have told Bajpai? She hugged me for a very long minute, Shilpa.

'When did you get out and when did you get in?'

Now how was I going to answer that one? I told her so. 'How did you leave jail and when?'

'Took a tonga, what else? Rickshaw-pullers have run away, not tongawalahs. How could they leave their horses to die? They gave me back my purse with the house keys intact.'

'Experience.' I noticed that she too was nodding.

I couldn't agree more. You go through life experiencing experience. She walked across and drew the curtains shut. 'Why?' I asked. She couldn't believe my question and carried her forefinger to her temples. Hmmm. More people could be thinking the same, wondering about my frame of mind, when I let go at the constable. Why do we say 'frame' of mind Mama. It should be state of mind, isn't it?

'What's gone wrong with you, Seema? Are you totally out of your mind?'

'Out of my mind, that's it. A much better phrase.'

She passed or rather waved her hand across my eyes. 'Where do you get lost, Seema? Which world are you in?'

She couldn't have noticed that I was also talking to my mother. I saw alarm on her face. When people get alarmed about you, it's time to get a hold of yourself. 'I will get a hold on myself, Shilpa, don't worry.'

'And what do you mean by that?'

'Getting a hold on myself?'

'What else?'

'Shilpa, it's like clutching the gathers of an ankle-length skirt, or shall we say a *lehnga*, its hem trailing on the floor. Getting a hold on yourself is something akin to that, isn't it?'

I noticed the incredulous look had not left her face, nor the dregs of disgust. 'Get me some chai, will you.' We sat down and had chai. I told her about meeting Alfie, the foreign correspondent. '*Christian Science Monitor*, you mean.' How does she know everything? 'He's writing very acerbically, you know,' and she added, after sipping her tea, 'will come to grief. Keep away from him.'

'What can they do to a firang? White skin, British passport, even if you throw him out, the police will need a good car to escort him to the airport.'

'Yes Seema, but they can keep him in the cooler for some days till the immigration or the emigration babus get their act together. Do you know, the babus are keener to get into emigration than immigration these days? More money in it.'

I keep quiet, no point in getting into an argument with her, she's bound to win, bloody know-all. 'How do you know all this, Shilpa?'

'I keep my ears open, absorb what is buzzing around me. You seem to be in a trance these days. Are you in love, or if I may say so, out of it?' I told her not to be stupid. We got down to discussing politics, Shilpa started it. 'There's no hope now, for the moment I mean. We don't have a party, what is worse, we don't even have an ideology to match this female. She is for the poor, she says, and the poor believe her. We have the Swatantra types, whom you will not approve of—starched kurta, starched leggings, hush puppies, tea served by bearers in china, serviettes in silver rings, and contempt for the government dripping from their thin lips in accented English. How can these blokes ever have a mass following? Or, and what a choice, you have the shakhawalahs.'

I know of her dislike for the Jana Sangh. 'You have the communists,' I said quietly. 'I knew you'd say that. They are with Mrs G, don't you see. And God save us from their ideology—demagoguery, revolution, class collaboration, trade unions, strikes, gheraos, encircle the top man, factory manager (in case you want more pay for no work) or the vice chancellor (if you want no exams or no invigilation so that you can copy). Surround him and don't let the bugger sneak off to the loo. Once he can't retain his piddle anymore, he will succumb.'

'You are quick to hate, to dismiss. And I don't mind the shakhas at all. They are cadre-based, disciplined youth, don't scoff at them. They can resist the lady. I appreciate cadres, there's a collective will about them and they can stand their ground.'

'Knew you'd say that, the communists too have cadres.'

'All the same I respect the shakhawalahs. We need all types.'

'Yes, but what about their brahmastras? The parmanu bumb as they call it, the science behind it came from Vedic lore, they copied the brahmastra, Oppie and co. Enola Gay was obviously the *udan khatola* of yore. And if Hanuman could burn Colombo and Galle with the flaming end of his tail, what are these Brits and Americans crowing about incendiary bombs?' I was about to enter into a boxing match with her, when the phone rang mercifully. It was Nishant. 'You are back, wish I had been told.' His tone was soft, not accusatory.

'Yes. Thought I'd let you know once I arrived here. The rains were getting a bit much too much for me in Kangra and the bed room had started leaking—all sorts of troubles.'

'I can't believe it, you travel and I don't know where you are or where you're off to. Someone asks me where you are, I say Kangra, and you could be in Dharamsala or Dalhousie or bloody Bakhloh!'

'Don't shout.' He immediately started pleading. 'Come to Delhi. Just leave Lucknow for God's sake. Don't enter the bloody place. It is crawling with these sleuths, CID, Special Branch…'

I butted in. 'What is so special about this branch?'

'They are the dedicated political intelligence types, you should know, you are a journalist. Who made you a journalist?' He was beside himself with fury. This, too, I had been hearing since that encounter with bloody, sneering Alfie.

'And you've been in the cooler. Two days there. If word

gets around I'll be booted out of my job. I am in the PMS—deputy secretary, bit of an underling, kicked around but so what, it happens to be the Prime Minister's Sectariat!'

'Secretariat.'

'Thanks for correcting me, Seema. But just vanish from Lucknow, please. Kangra must have bored you, should have bored you by now. Don't go back. Come to Delhi. A new house is being readied for us.Or how about a few days with your uncle?'

He meant my maternal uncle, Balbir chacha—the one who could put me wise to a lot of goings on concerning my parents. I nodded, Shilpa laughed.'Well what do you have to say about it?' he screamed.

'Can't you see I agree?' Shilpa shouted loud at that and cried out, 'she was nodding'.'Who was that, Shilpa?' 'Yes,' I answered. He laughed. 'Who told you I was in the cooler?' I was serious and my tone cold. He sensed it. Was he snooping?

Work; the very thought of it weighs you down. Adjacent to the Residency we have a mango orchard—trees mostly of the Langra variety. The caretaker, Mushtaq Mian, what has he been doing? He hasn't even come to offer his *salaam*s, meaning to meet me. We belong to old Lucknow—we don't meet people, we offer salaams, or regard, and to the much older, respect; our tawaifs were more cultured than the middle class housewives you find today, hunting on tired legs for a bargain deal, a machine embroidered kurta, we wouldn't look at. Anything which looks like the real thing and is not the real thing, but can pass off as the real thing, they will go in for, as long as it is cheap! I thought of the mangoes for the first time this evening, in months. Were there dry winds in early March, was the mango blossom blown away, I hadn't even cared to find out. June is the peak season for the Langra. Mama, I remember once father asked you, 'What kind of a girl have we brought up?' I am asking myself something similar today. Fortunately we have a few Fazri trees, the ones with the huge fruit, very sweet and sticky, but with no particular taste of its own.

Suddenly I hear the light splash of water. Bless him, the Bhishti is here with his *mashq*, water skin, and the smell of wet earth rises, its fragrance better than all the perfumeries of Kanauj. He is bent low as always, the leather mashq almost tied to his back. I have always called him Mashq Mian, no matter how you scolded me, Mama. I call him the same now and we laugh, both of us. 'How are you, Najeeb Mian?' I ask. He shakes his head, 'No, Mashq Mian.' And we laugh again. I ask him if he has been paid. Not for a year, he replies. I left some money with Mushtaq, I tell him. He simply shakes his head. I go in, dig into my purse and hand over what is due to him. I sleep well at night. Tomorrow, I'll go to the orchard.

Rabia

It is early morning, a lingering dawn-light still visible when I get up, throw open the living room windows and step out, observe the damp on the grass, rain drops still lingering on the bougain vine. I had almost forgotten the almond tree, the leaves would turn into crinkled ochre, now and then even the colour of oxblood as they drifted down one by one at the slightest touch of breeze in March. I once asked, you had woken up late, how old the tree was, when was it planted, and you answered 'in the past'. How old is the past, Mama? Can I turn into a child again and ask you this?

The rain must have stopped quite some time earlier because I watch morning joggers huffing and puffing, and splashing in a puddle or two. Then I spot Rabia and Zaira, old school friends and classmates; I wave to them, a cup of chai in one hand. They are thrilled to see me. We can hardly believe it's you, they say, as they walk in and squat on the cane chairs in the veranda.

'No pea fowl?' asks Rabia, laughing. That's the past again, but the near past.

'They don't know I am back, word hasn't got through. I haven't seen any koels either in the last three days.'

'I remember a peahen which foraged around picking up

insects. She had gawky legs, an awkward sort of a bird.' That was Zaira. Rabia got her chance. 'There was a peacock here too but he has shifted to Delhi.' Much laughter, I notice.

'Yes, would love some of Fauzia's cardamom tea,' says Zaira in answer to my query. On cue, Fauzia brings in the *ilaichi* chai in steaming mugs. We start reminiscing, happens when old friends from school are together. We were a gang, Shilpa, Rabia, Daksha and I. Zaira was on the fringes. Rabia was completely laid back, not bothered about exams, coming late to class often because she had overslept. Her house was too close to a mosque and she used to tell us that the 4 a.m. call to prayer, the azaan, would not just wake her up but even rattle the glass in her window panes. I always stood up for the azaan, it sounded sonorous, almost musical. You say that because you have never heard it at four in the morning, she would shout back. Her one ambition was to move out of the house, and out of Golaganj. Her grandfather was a wastrel and blew away all the family money gambling. She told us that he once lost a bet of one thousand silver coins on a single cock fight. She always pronounced it as a 'rooster fight' and we would rag her. 'Why not a cock fight, Rabia?' And she would blush. The father was sedate and ran an optics shop in the Qaiserbagh Chowk.

'Remember when we were taken to see an English film at the Novelty Cinema in Lalbagh. Our English mistress was chaperoning us. Each time the "fuck" word was uttered, almost before it was uttered, she'd shout "Beep!" We couldn't stop giggling.'

I want to test the waters. 'Has it been as bad in Lucknow as it is in Delhi? I am talking of the Emergency.' Zaira answers, 'It is the worst in Haryana.'

I probe further. 'If Raj Narayan had not filed that election petition, nothing of the kind would have happened. There would have been no forced sterilization, no firing at Turkman Gate, no jail for politicians. What do you say?'

Rabia couldn't restrain herself. 'O, so Indira would have kept ruling for ever, is it? No setback, no disqualification.' Then she whispered, 'Do you know Raj Narayan was paid by Sanjay Gandhi to file an election petition? Don't laugh, his logic was that when Mrs Gandhi is disqualified, she can declare an Emergency and lock up all her enemies or opponents (they mean the same thing in politics). That was the scheme.'

I was laughing but Zaira piped up. 'There could be something in this rumour. Indira would be disqualified, so Sanjay could have calculated that he takes over from her, simple. How else can he become PM? Such things can happen in our country.'

Rabia was a great believer in conspiracies. I remember her vociferous defence of Lee Harvey Oswald in school. He was either hired or forced by Vice President Lyndon Johnson to kill JFK. What else could the poor fellow do, things of that sort. And she had said Oswald was merely a scapegoat. We never let her live that down. Children can be cruel and our gang and I were no exceptions. I was wondering why they hadn't mentioned my time in the cooler. They haven't been in touch with Shilpa, I think to myself, for they don't mention a thing about my jail sortie. 'You've been living apart for a year now, haven't you?' Rabia's tone was concerned, slightly accusatory, as if it was my fault.

'We have been meeting though, we stayed together for a week in Kangra. He took some leave. Will be tough now, though.' Rabia questions with her big lustrous eyes, the eyebrows lifted and the gaze unremitting. 'He has moved to the PM's Secretariat.' Normally people would have jumped at the news and there would have been a lot of hugs, eyes teary with emotion. How times change. Rabia's eyes turned serious, they were always a mirror to her soul. 'Someone needs to talk to you seriously, Seema, for an entire morning. You need a session with a counsellor.' Zaira was always good at adding her two bits. 'Someone who will talk to you for a week and put sense in your head.'

'Oh, so you have heard from Shilpa,' I said. They were non-committal. Rabia said, 'I thought you were still in the cooler.' Zaira added, 'That's why we were so delighted to see you here, in your house.' Hmm. I prepared for being lectured to. Rabia spoke. 'The earlier you get out of this place the better. At the moment there's nothing for you here. It's another thing that there's nothing here for anyone, but that shouldn't worry you. Just get out, and don't head for Kangra this time. Take the train to Delhi. *Kya rakha hai Kangra main?* Some rocks, an old fort, Pahari paintings older than the fort, what's in it for you? You leave Nishant alone for a year! You think there are no girls in Delhi?' Zaira was not slow to add, 'Delhi is full of such girls.'

Hmm, so that was the spin, I found myself nodding. Take care of husband's hormones—prime wifely duty, must be a chapter in the shastras on the subject, or certainly in Manu Smriti, the one which tells us, along with *chamars* and sundry SCs, not to ever recite the sacred *Gayatri*.

'And you have to look after his job'—that was Zaira.

'I thought he was paid to look after his job. Salry and purk, as Punjabis put it.'

'Don't be ridiculous, Seema. You can't go speaking out

against the Emergency with Nishant in Delhi.' I butted in, 'But you do the same, Rabia. If we can't speak openly, at least we can amongst ourselves.'

'You are being stubborn, by which I mean stupid! Once word gets around, Nishant will be in trouble. And if he is in trouble, so are you. The two of you are not going to find it easy.' Rabia was done, but Zaira had to speak up as always. 'First Shilpa gets involved and now you.' I found Rabia looking daggers at Zaira. What was all this? What did they want to keep from me?

'Who or what is Shilpa involved with?' There was silence from both, but I could not forget the accusatory glance Rabia had given her friend. I persisted and after much persuasion got them to come out with something. 'She is involved with a journalist.'

'Not a foreign journalist?' I asked almost intuitively. There was no answer. 'Not involved with Alfie, is she?'

'Who is Alfie?'

'Alfred Hemmings of the *Christian Science Monitor*.'

'How do you know about him Seema?'

'Do I? I know this guy very cursorily. And is Shilpa involved with him politically or you know what…?'

'*Tobah*, *tobah*! What dirty thoughts, Seema.'

'Is she sleeping with him?'

At this they got up and left without even giving me a hug. I would never get an answer to that one. But the maali told me in the afternoon that the police had visited Shilpaji. Well well.

It was quite sticky when I went to the mango grove. Word had spread. Mushtaq Mian was waiting for me, an umbrella in his hand to shield me from the sun which had come out for a few hours. He handed me hundred-odd rupees—the poor sales of the langra mangoes. I didn't argue, asked about the Fazri crop, yes I could see them drooping from the branches. He plucked a few and put them in a cane basket padded with straw. I asked him why the Bhishti wasn't paid. No money. Pesticides were needed for the mango trees, he said. In fact, that was why the langra crop was poor. Send these mangoes home, I told him as I asked for an auto rickshaw and visited the Residency. In any case, if you live in Qaiserbagh, you can't keep away from the Residency. A city changes in a year, I found it crowded with ochre coloured Vespa scooters, newly named as Bajaj scooters. Why the ochre colour? What hold had our swamis on Italy? They were all emitting a fairly foul smoke. A hoarding or two I found interesting. One read, 'Are you in problem? Call and get solution.' Yet, most things remained the same. People, both the well-to-do through their car windows and the common man, spat out their sepia dribble as if from a soda siphon. At the Imambara, I found the three-domed Asifi mosque looking a muddy grey without plaster or paint. In the Residency grounds couples were cuddling and kissing away, as always, where else could they go? In the museum there wasn't a word on Havelock and almost nothing on Henry Lawrence except the spot where he was shot. The write-ups both in the museum and on pillars were a disappointment. On the Brits standing up to the besieging Indian soldiers, there wasn't a word. I am no historian but can confidently say that one of our eternal passions is to play with history. I went past a roofless Banqueting Hall constructed by Nawab Sadat Ali Khan—spacious saloons, silk dewans, chandeliers, mirrors. Found a stucco fireplace somewhere. Was surprised to find that Indian soldiers had also fought for the

British here. There was a memorial to them which talked of soldiers from 'Guzerat, Mysore and Punjab' and the 'devoted gallantry and fidelity of the native officers and sepoys of the Hon. Companies 13th Battalion Native Infantry who fell during the defence of Lucknow.'

❁

Bipin Kumar came over in the evening. My fatigue disappeared. Bipin was a classmate of Nishant's in college. They were quite close then. He never tried for the services, went into law, did a stint with a solicitor in London after his LLM and practised at the Lucknow branch of the Allahabad High Court. But Delhi was the place where you made a name—and money. He started with a small *khoka* in the High court next to the Jaipur House and was now mostly practising there, though he had been also sited at Tees Hazari courts infrequently. He could crack a good joke, good sincere friend of Nishant. 'What a pleasure Bipin! What brings you here?'

'What a pleasure Seema, what brings you here? Some of us would wish you were in Kangra?'

'Who is us?'

'Me and Nishant.'

'Hmm, so you are not happy seeing me, want me tucked away in the hills.'

'Away from the law, Seema.' And he laughed.

'Yes, the bloody law is trying to bind me down, I'll soon suffer from rope-burn.'

'Not any more. You are free from the ropes now. In fact, if I could pun a little, we had to pull ropes.'

'Who's we, Bipin? Your pronouns confuse me at times.'

'Same old team Seema, Nishant and me.'

'Not you alone?'

He shook his head. 'He phones people and you do the foot slog?'

'That's about it. Someone has to make the physical approach before such things are put to rest. Verbal orders followed by paper which moves from police to prosecutor to magistrate who finally discharges the accused. A bit circumlocutory.'

'You were always good with words Bipin, that circumlocutory bit sounded nice, thanks a lot. I owe you something better than this chai but I never offer drinks when Nishant is not around.'

'I didn't come for a drink, just came around to tell you the good news.'

'Yes it's a great relief. You are in Delhi now most of the time, I hear. Are you practising at Tees Hazari?' I wanted to put him down a bit. He wasn't happy. 'I practise at the High Court, Seema. Tees Hazari has Sessions courts, District judges and the like.' I apologized dutifully but I was now off to tease him. 'What is the world coming to Bipin, doctors and police ganging up to commit forcible vasectomies; and one can't even slap a constable!' I laughed to indicate I was joking. He didn't laugh.

'Don't try it again Seema, or you could be in the cooler for three years. And this time we may not be able to bail you out.'

'Bail? Am I out on bail?'

'No, Seema, for heaven's sake. The case has been dropped, you are free.'

'You mean till I slap the next cop.' We both laughed as he took his leave.

A Visitor

I hear a knock on the door, somewhat indistinct.

Or are my anxieties playing the *tabalchi* tap-tapping on my eardrums? Aural bloody hallucination? Have things come to this? It is ten at night, dash it and I am listening to the BBC. I switch off my transistor and wait. Some seconds later the knock comes through again.

Can't be the police—their knuckles are more aggressive, knuckle-dusters rather and the boots are hob-nailed, don't I know? They would have kicked the door open by now. This seems like a fugitive knock. I switch on the light in the veranda and open the door. It is Alfie.

'I thought you were under arrest!'

'O, you heard that, did you? Well I gave them the slip. And why did you have to switch on the veranda light for God's sake!'

'How was I to know it was you? I first thought of a police raid, dismissed the thought immediately, the police would have been more audible. Like a blunderbuss.'

I notice he is nodding again, but this time I am not infuriated. 'And you were listening to the BBC,' he smiles.

'You could hear that standing in the veranda?'

'Yes, the night heard you beyond the boundary wall. Play

the BBC softer I suggest.' And as an afterthought he adds, 'and who told you I was in the cooler?'

Didn't I ask Nishant the very same question a day back, or was it two days? 'Shilpa.'

He nods. Shilpa had rung me up some two hours earlier to say he had been arrested. I ask Alfie if he has had anything to eat. He shakes his head. I move to the fridge. All that's left of my dinner is bitter gourd and some chickpeas, the chicken I have gobbled up. I whip up an omelette. Many thanks, he says, but asks me to turn off the dining room light. I'll eat in the kitchen, he tells me. That's where servants eat, I tell him.

'Fugitives and pressmen have eaten in worse places. This is a treat. Thanks.'

He is obviously staying for the night. I don't even bother to ask. Hope he goes away early in the morning before the maid comes in, hope the milkman doesn't see him slinking away, how mean can I be, Mama, but then what would she think if she saw him in pyjamas in the morning, the maid I mean? He tells me about his escapade. He goes to Amausi, the airport that is, and the cabbie tells him 'Lot of police sahib, some big sahib is coming.' Alfie becomes dramatic here as he enacts the scene. 'I duck, don't want to be seen. Turn around. He thinks he has misheard me. Turn around! I shout again, *wapas*. The bloody big sahib is me, intuition tells me. This isn't protocol, with flag cars lined up, and big wigs sauntering around slapping their batons on their calves. This is the constabulary out to get me, Sub-inspectors with their red-and-khaki side-caps. He takes me to his house, the cabbie, where else can I hide. We had cruised past the Carlton Hotel where I had stayed, crawling with police again. I take the cabbie's hospitality, have a cup of hot chai with him, but can't tax him further. He'll be in trouble once they get to know. Later he leaves me at Qaiserbagh Chowk—should be called a circle, I feel. I sit there with an optician for an hour, and then move here. I'll be gone early tomorrow.'

I take him to the guest room and ask him to help me fix a new sheet on the bed there. I can't hold myself any longer and brashly tell him, 'I thought your nocturnal hideouts were at Shilpa's?'

'O, you have heard that one also?' He nods. 'So you keep yourself abreast of scandal,' nods again. 'How come you were a zero with the Emergency?'

We move to the living room. We are speaking softly—you spoke softly those days—as we shift to the living room, where I switch on the table lamp and turn off the other lights.

'I can't imagine her doing all this, Alfie. She has done so much for the environment, for things that are right, look at how she struggled for Mujib and Bangladesh. And whatever pro-poor measures she has taken can't be cynically dismissed as something she did for grabbing votes. Can't imagine how she could do it.' He did not choose to answer.

'How long do you think this will last?' I ask.

'I should be asking you, Seema. If the army sides with her, this emergency could go on for a very long time.'

'Army? How does the army come in Alfie? You goras are hung up on military takeovers. This is not Pakistan. India is different.'

'How different? You're the same people, aren't you? That's what you've been saying all along, especially when you whine about India being torn into two. Bharat Mata sundered. When it comes to an army takeover, you suddenly become different. How come?'

I explain as best as I can—talk about pathans and their swagger—the Ayub Khans et al, the poor politicians Pakistan always had—and don't forget Jinnah didn't go to jail for a single day, while Nehru spent ten years there. We had much better politicians. And we didn't rig elections the way Bhutto did. But why do you say it will last forever?

'I didn't say that, but the way people and politicians have succumbed, judges, journalists, the lot, she could go on till she thinks Sanjay is mature enough to step into her sandals.' I answered, 'Which could be never.'

'I wouldn't say that. Worse people than Sanjay have ascended thrones in the past and won at the hustings in the present. And look at the way people cheer for trains running on time. They think it's a value. It has always been the dictatorship mantra, roads sparklingly clean, trams on time, conductors in clean khaki.'

'You think she could change the Constitution, make it presidential and force the president to sign the decree? That could happen, Mr Hemmings.'

'Why not? And let me tell you there are many people in the country with presidential ambitions. No dearth of wannabe dictators in the country.'

'Punjabi trait, isn't it? She is surrounded by that coterie now. To follow your line of argument, the next dictator could come from Punjab, unbridled power is a lust growing in the land of the five rivers.'

'He could come from anywhere Seema—Maharashtra, Gujarat.'

'Or like Savarkar, from the Andamans. You know Alfie, I am not too happy joining you in this Emergency bashing.'

'Why?'

'There's this lingering reek of colonialism, you berating what's happening to us. Some of you always said we would bungle things. Your "Koi Hai" types who would simply shout and the native khansama would come running must be licking their chops.'

'That was forty years ago. No one thinks like that anymore.'

Next morning I found him hesitating at the door. 'I was thinking of requesting you for something, but have thought better of it.' Why can't you speak out, I told him, and soon regretted making the offer.

'You may be wondering why I came here at all. I have friends in the city, was once here with the British Council Library. I have a packet with me to be delivered to Shambhu Nath. Remember the ironmonger whose shop they were sealing. He is in hiding. I have a packet, actually two, to be delivered to him, one envelope is from London. I could have asked at least three others I can think of at the moment to act as my couriers. I don't want to keep the package with me, for who can tell when I am nabbed. Wouldn't want to be caught with this thing on my hands. This would give them further proof of my treachery and my involvement with runaway fugitives. Moreover this package contains money, feel it, it's a fat envelope, the kind in-laws give in dowry. If I am caught with it your Broadcasting Ministry will say the CIA was flooding India with money to create trouble. The dread of the foreign hand is a part of the lady's psyche, it is not put on. If this fear had not been put into her by her socialist colleagues and the Intelligence Bureau, you may not have had the Emergency. So will you deliver it to the fellow?'

I pointed to the envelope and asked, 'Is this from his wife?' 'No,' he answered, 'she died some months back. It's from his brother, a bit of an oddball, but a diehard Jana Sanghi, goes by the name of Ram Dollar Pande. Don't laugh, he changed "Dulare" into Dollar, easier to pronounce by us goras, isn't it? He lives in Wembley and has a string of properties in Gravesend. The money is from him and there's a letter of support from the party.'

'How much is in that envelope, Alfie?'

'Frankly I don't know, but was told there's a hell of a lot. Someone I know brought it from Wembley to me. This Ram Dollar Pande was my landlord in Wembley. I lived in a rented flat for three years.' So I asked where he, friend and night-visitor Alfie, fitted into all this. What is the Jana Sangha to you? 'Nothing,' he answered, 'but they are people who can resist the Dictatorni.' We laughed, though it was a tense moment for me. Then I spoke up, 'Are you mad, Alfie? I can't be seen getting into all this, I'm married to a civil servant, an upright really civil guy. And you want me to go haring after criminals and carrying money for them!'

'They are not criminals, and you need to pay for the sins of your ignorance.'

'What the hell do you mean?'

'Ignorance of the black deeds of the Lady.'

'She has put you all in your place, hasn't she—Nixon and Henry and all the rest. But tell me where's this fellow's hideout? How do I look for the bum?' He gave me a Faizabad Road address and a telephone number, and emphasized that he was hiding with a Christian family. He went out and I kept looking at his back as he finally disappeared without meeting the milkman or the newspaper guy, the one who hurls the rubber-band-bound paper from across the boundary wall. I pride myself with being one of those half a dozen people who read the *Pioneer.* Looked forward to the paper by habit, though the papers were bedraggled and shabby looking, bereft of all worthwhile news.

Come dusk and I put through a call at the number given. A lady with a funny accent answered the phone. '*Kaun bolta*?' she said in a sort of a voice which indicated that she was reluctant to answer the call. I put on as much of an accent as I could and asked is that Mrs Margaret Handscomb? I got no answer, so before she could put down the phone I said I am a friend of a journalist and have to deliver a letter. I'll be there in half an hour, and I put down the phone before she could ask further questions or protest. I came out, walked a bit and then took a rickshaw. First thing I asked him was to put on the hood, gave him the address and pushed off. Noticing how the houses were numbered, I got down some twenty paces earlier and paid off the rickshaw guy. I rang the bell and pushed my way through a swing door to find a clothesline in a small walled-in space. After a minute the woman who had spoken to me on the phone came out, I could spot her through her accent. She must have been around forty and was good looking, except for the grim expression that swept over her face when she saw me. I handed over the package and the letter. 'Who are you?' she asked. 'Don't worry, I am a friend. You know who this is for, don't you? I was there when his shop was sealed. Give it to him.'

'Just hold on till I give him the package,' she said and walked in. She came out in a minute, saying he wants a word with you. I shook my head, 'some other time,' I said, and gave her a friendly nod as I walked out.

The Oracle

I made some tea for myself next morning and waited for Fauzia who had been with our family for some years. We had hired her when mother fell seriously ill, never to recover. She did not turn up. At night there was a knock again—too much of a good thing I thought, two bloody nights in a row. What were things coming to? This time I was bold, hadn't been listening to the BBC. Ironic commentary on our times, isn't it Mama? I opened the door heroically. It was Aslam, Fauzia's husband, with their daughter who must have just moved into her teens. He looked shaken. 'What has happened, Aslam?' I asked.

'They have taken Fauzia away, Mem Sahib.'

'They' had become the standard pronoun for Police recently. I took them in and made them sit on two slightly tattered poufs. 'There were two women with the party.' Witnesses, I said to myself. Our advanced Uttar Pradesh still didn't have a policewoman in its ranks. That meant they had come for Fauzia specifically. Quite intriguing. What could she have done to invite this?

'Is she at the police station?'

'I went there, but no one was willing to talk to me, Mem Sahib.'

'Why have they taken her away, answer me, Aslam Mian? I can't think of a reason. Is it a criminal case?' I suddenly thought of someone plonking stolen property at their ramshackle hutment in Gola Ganj, next to the Baroodkhana. There was no answer, he was confused, he said. So was I, but I read his eyes and didn't like what I saw. He was hiding something. He said my daughter will work for you. A child working for me! I politely declined. 'I will wait for Fauzia,' I told him. He insisted. 'Keep her with you,' he said. 'She can't stay alone in an outhouse, Aslam Mian. What is wrong with you?'

'She'll sleep in the kitchen,' he said. 'What's her name?' I asked. 'Elham' he answered. She will not work, I made it clear to him. 'But I want her books, she will study, you understand?' He smiled, she has brought her books, they are in this basta, the school bag.

I took a good look at Elam, she stared back, unafraid—black tresses, big brown eyes, no ornament of any kind around her wrist or neck, no colyrium, no nail polish. She spoke to my heart. I took her to the guest room. Next morning I found her asleep on the living room carpet. When I came out after a shower, I found her with a broom cleaning up a termite trail extending from a window sill. How come I had not noticed the termites? No, I wasn't going to give her back to Fauzia easily. Remember Mama I asked you once what 'Ton' means and you gave me a weird look which seemed to ask what was wrong with me? Well I had heard the mother shout at Elham, *'Haiza, Ton khaye tujhe!'* May cholera and plague eat you up. That's how they curse.

I got the store room cleaned, put a cot there and she was housed, if I may put it that way. I went out to Hazrat Ganj and bought some interesting books for children, ones with pictures and diagrams—they would speak to her. I was soon to discover she was torn between Urdu and Hindi and did not know either well enough. Next morning, against the shrill advice of Shilpa, I phoned the police station. 'I have heard that you have arrested my maid servant Fauzia, Aslam Khan's wife.' He interrupted me saying, '*Aapne galat suna hai*', you have been informed wrongly. I persisted, 'Under which sections have you arrested her?' 'We just told you no one by that name has been arrested.'

Me: 'You could have brought her in for interrogation, *pooch taach*. Her husband told me.'

Police Station: 'Madam, he must have divorced her, or sent her back to her parents, or killed her. Who knows?' And the guy put the phone down.

The next evening Shilpa phoned. Apparently a delegation of foreign correspondents met Minister V.C. Shukla of the Information and Broadcasting Ministry, concerned over the disappearance of Alfie. Shukla stoutly denied that there had been any move to arrest 'the accredited correspondent of the *Christian Science Monitor*, Mr Alfred Hemming.' But he went on to warn 'certain misguided visiting pressmen to be careful about what they report, and not believe rumours spread by anonymous, mischievous anti-national elements.' They were anonymous, these sources, because they didn't have the courage to speak up. They chose instead 'the nefarious route of the whispering gallery to serve their malicious ends.' He warned the pressmen that they should not take the kindness and hospitality of the Indian government for granted, and 'action would be taken at the first hint of malice and falsity discovered in any despatch.' When asked about the whereabouts of Mr Alfred Hemming, the minister, tall fair and handsome V.C. Shukla, stated that the 'I&B Ministry did not keep tabs on the locations of foreign or local correspondents. India was a free country. You could walk where you liked and talk what you liked.' 'He could have added that the ministry would sock you where and when it liked, I thought,' said Shilpa over the phone. At the end of the minister's speech there was a flutter of applause which sounded like a wet bird taking reluctant flight at the approach of a luminously speckled cobra. Shilpa could be nasty. She had heard all this on the BBC, and as she was putting the phone down, said 'Thank God'. Now where did that come from?

I noticed that Fauzia's daughter was unhappy stirring out. When the vegetable vendor came and squatted on the veranda, a Kachi by the name of Purshotam, Elham would not come out to carry the veggies to the kitchen. I let it pass. Then the maali, the part time gardener, wanted to buy some seedlings—rains were the time to sow—and she was reluctant to come out and hand him the money I gave her. The gardener was a Kahar, people who carried the village brides in palkis or palanquins as the Brits termed them. Village brides now went by bus to the husband's mud-and-thatch homestead. Kahars had to look for other occupations. It was the maali who told me later that Fauzia would soon be released. He knew a Kahar constable at the police station. They had caught the wrong woman.

Next morning Rabia dropped by, Rabia of lustrous eyes that darted right and left as if to warn her of an attack. She was startled to see Elham. I want to tell you something, she whispered in English—didn't want Elham to listen. She asked

Elham what her name meant, and the girl didn't know. She turned to me and said 'inspired', that's what the name means in Arabic. Then she came out with the story. There was a reading of the Qoran at Afreeda's house. Qorankhwani, it is called. They had a son born in the family. The maids and servants were welcome. And as the reading was near ending this chit of a girl with dazed eyes and her torso swinging this way and that shouted 'Indira Gandhi will be in jail next year!' She said a few other things too, but most of it was unintelligible. Imagine the shock! The Qorankhwani broke up and there were people who didn't even wait for the halwa and the eats, as they moved off! They ran for ekka, auto, car—anything to get away fast. A bit of a disaster for Afreeda's family and she laughed. 'Elham fainted and they had to carry her home.'

'It was a fit, wasn't it?'

'Of course it was, Seema. You say the most obvious things sometimes.'

It made sense. So whoever 'sang' to the cops was not present in the room, and garbled information reached the police station. Mother got arrested and threatened instead of the daughter. 'Keep her safe,' said Rabia, as she walked away. 'Hope what she said comes true,' and we both laughed.

Fauzia was let off and I expected her anytime. She walked in at twilight. Before opening the door I looked out of the window and didn't like what I saw. Aslam was peeping over the wall. Why couldn't he come in with her? 'Sorry Fauzia, you've had a rough time. I hope you were not treated too badly at the police station. I didn't come there personally but I phoned them up.'

'I was near the phone then Mem Sahib, *shukriya*.' I noticed the child had not come out to greet her mother. I wanted to ask Fauzia how she wanted to go about things now, but refrained. 'Mem Sahib I will take Elham back, thanks for keeping her.' I was not sure I wanted to part with the kid. Why had Aslam stayed back outside the compound? What if Fauzia handed over the girl to the cops? Had Fauzia made a deal with them? The police must be bloody worried—an oracular utterance, a *vaani*, sending the prime minister to jail!

'What are you going to do with her, Fauzia, bring her in touch with the police?'

'Never! *Lakwa maar jaye mujhe* [May paralysis hit me] before a thing like that happens. She's my daughter, born off my womb!' The excitement in her voice drained off suddenly as she added, 'I will show her to a *peer.*'

I didn't want any of that, a peer meant an exorcist. I sensed what could happen, some long haired fake from a dargah in Lucknow, if not farther off from Bansa or Dewa Sharif, the two Muslim shrines in nearby Barabanki, muttering mumbo jumbo in Arabic, accompanied by bad music and perhaps even a drum. And he would give the kid a good thrashing—how else would the demon that possessed her be excised?

'No Fauzia, I know what your peer and everyone else in the lane will inflict on her. She will become a spectacle, with people watching as if they were in a cinema theatre. Some rogue will make a fool of you all, strip you of money, brush the child with a whisk or a broom, mumble a fake prayer perhaps in fake Arabic and give her a beating. Can't let that happen. I will show her to a doctor, she needs care, not blows. There is no *bhoot* (spirit) inhabiting her.' Of course there were recriminations, tears, loud protestations, the saving grace being she did not tear her hair. I made the daughter meet the mother, gave Fauzia some money and sent her off.

Doctor Sushima Misra of the Balrampur Hospital said it is puberty, onset of the hormonal swirl, as she dubbed it. It will pass in another year hopefully she said. Give her a sedative when she gets a fit like this. I wasn't there, doctor. I am not fully certain if it was a fit. But I verified from those who were there that she did not froth at the mouth. Doctor nodded, keep me informed she said and sent us off.

Rabia and Shilpa had started calling Elham 'Indira Vani'. It became sort of a joke among friends. The first time they thought it up they couldn't stop giggling. The tirades from my husband had softened. I couldn't come to Delhi because the house he was going to move into was getting renovated. There was no insistence on me being sent back to Kangra to complete my book.

I had brought interesting books for children and got Elham interested in them. One was a story book on an aquarium, with lovely pictures, except one where an ugly big fish was swallowing a smaller one. There was a full page illustration of a fish skeleton. One story was drenched with our *desi* sentimentality, the small fish being chased by an ugly blunt-nosed and doubtlessly bigger one gets hold of a mantra that can crack the huge glass aquarium. She could escape, but she refrains from chanting the glass-cracking mantra, thinking of all the other fish that will die or fry, I don't fully remember Mama. Elham's eyes had turned watery. The radio had talked of a stampede at a temple. I explained the word stampede as best as I could, and translated it as '*bhedia dhasan*' (sheep scampering away from wolf). The number of casualties, especially the dead, was not mentioned—nothing bad was supposed to happen during the Emergency, and nothing did, if you were to believe the TV and radio. (Our TV was in Delhi, so I made do with the Philips radio.)

Two days later on a Sunday, Elham brought in drama in the morning, mime, nightmare, a bit of liturgy thrown in, all enacted in a surreal performance, if I could call it that. She mimed the breast stroke that stood for someone swimming. Then in a high-pitched voice, which didn't sound like her own, she said a huge fish skeleton swam its way to the shore (she couldn't have an idea what a beach looks like). A crowd had gathered, hawkers, ice cream vendors, boys selling balloons. Fishermen clustered around and argued what fish it could be. Then someone in the crowd spotted its eyes, it still had eyes intact and was watching the crowd, and when some fool stamped hard and threatened her, she shifted her snout towards him. Then the crowd ran screaming, some were crushed while others were drowned in the sea. Her face had turned pale. I slapped her and threw a glass of cold water on her face. She came to. I hugged her.

I tried calling the doctor but she was not there and the operator put me through to the head of the Psychiatry Department of Balrampur Hospital. He had been briefed by Dr Sushima Misra, he said. He must have been busy for as I took time to narrate the entire saga, he butted in saying, 'She's your *naukrani*, isn't she?' So much loaded in that one query. She's just a servant girl, so why are you so het up? 'She's not!' I screamed, but then when he asked so what is she, I had no answer.

Soon I was to find out this was just the first of a series. Dreams or hallucinations also come in series, like M.F. Husain's paintings on horses. Elham's dreams came cantering in. A camel skeleton crosses the border by mistake and walks into Pakistan; camel skeleton mind you, hump and bone intact. It terrifies the Rangers, for in the moonlight the camel turns luminescent. The glow can be observed for miles. What's even more frightening is that there are two large chunks of topaz in its eye sockets. Allah save us, cry the Rangers as they bolt, leaving bunker and armoury unguarded. It was a well thought out plan by the crafty Indians, the glow from the moonlit bones had lit up their post, the Rangers think. They wanted us to be sitting ducks, these Indians! As the Rangers flee, they leave this walking skeleton under a camel thorn tree. When they return next afternoon, they find that half the babul tree has been eaten up! Allah have mercy! Allah *raham kar!* They cry as they untie this structure of naked bones. The camel returns to India and the Border Security Force is horrified to find that there are drugs—bloody heroin—in the eye sockets! These Pakistanis will get hold of any device to smuggle drugs into India!

'*Haram ki aulad* (bastards)!' they shout at the Rangers, 'smuggling drugs are you? We won't touch them! And where are our topaz solitaires, you thieves?'

'And you were smuggling jewels, what of that? Trading in Kohinoors, you bloody dhotiwalahs.'

The whole day there was heavy artillery bombardment from both sides. Two goats were killed on the Indian side while thatch fires made Pakistani peasants abandon a hamlet. I have added my bit and amazing things get churned out in translations, but this sums up what Elham enacted.

❁

Nothing disappears forever, dregs are dregs and they have a habit of hanging on close to the bottom shelf. Images stamp themselves on the mind. That big blunt nosed fish has stayed with me. She floats in my dreams. And when I get up in the morning, I think of her as a floating object looking for a lost memory.

Nautanki Walah

Shilpa called. Come over Seema, Rabia is here and we have something interesting to tell you. I took an auto and went across. We had all been to the same school and class in Loreto Convent. Over a coffee I was told the news, Shilpa was bursting with it. A procession in support of the Emergency is going to be taken out tomorrow, believe it or not! It would be headed by Nirupam Khera, the principal actor in 'Ramnath Halwai Nautanki'. Trucks have been commandeered to bring in the slogan-shouting idiots. It is starting from the university and will end at Baradari. An order for fifty national flags has been placed with the Khadi Bhandar.

'Whose idea is this?'

'We believe it is Nirupam Khera's, fellow is harbouring political ambitions now. Don't you remember, Ramnath Halwai, best vegetarian restaurant in town, aloo gobi and matar paneer dripping with desi ghee? We took our Goel-and-Garg *bhenji*s there. Remember the end of Vanita's *chunni* landed in the buttermilk, and in her hurry to extricate it, the glass toppled and broke, table and floor covered with butter milk? You were there, Seema.'

Of course I was. Then disaster fell on the restaurant owner, the food inspectors raided and came away with reams of blotting paper. The income tax people had put them wise—had come across invoices. Nothing like blotting paper to add ballast to *khoya* sweets. The Ramnath Halwai Nautanki became Ramnath Galakandi Nautanki thereafter. Nirupam Khera had become its star 'actor', if you can use such a word for a *nautanki* hero.

Rabia said, 'Don't you remember the hit number?' I shook my head. Shilpa exclaimed, 'You've been out in the hills too long.' Then Rabia sang the ditty, shaking her body in the manner of nautanki dancers, placing her hand on her heart, as she sang:

launda patwari ka bada namkeen,
bada namkeen, hai bada namkeen!
launda patwari ka bada namkeen.

(The *patwari*'s son was very salty, the ditty basically said.) The number was sung by Nirupam's partner. A dispute arose between the two girls as to whether she was Nirupam's wife or not, but the argument remained unresolved.

The next day we were all there to watch the charade. Route and venue had been changed. The procession was now to start from the circle in front of the Assembly and move to the Aminuddaula Park, where stirring meetings and rallies had been held during British times. This time it was Rabia's car, but Barkat was driving. He was still underage and did not have a driving license. The crowd here was much more than we expected. Chaps were being unloaded from tempos and pickup trucks. Then two busses came in, one from Hardoi, another from Sitapur, and we saw hordes clambering down, all carrying banners praising Indiraji. Barkat suggested we move to the Aminuddaula Park, because once the procession started the crush would be impossible to navigate. There were many boys from the Youth Congress and plenty of *hai hai*s were being shouted. The crowd was already chanting slogans against the CIA and foreign correspondents. '*Videshi patrakaron ko / juthe maro salon ko*!' Foreign correspondents should be beaten with shoes. People were holding placards carrying similar slogans. One hoodlum, he looked like one, carried a banner which said 'down with indiscipline'. 'Mark Tully Bharat choro', 'Alfrud Humming Bharat choro'. I whispered to Shilpa asking her if Alfie was still hiding in her bedroom. She turned red, blood flowing to her cheeks. Rabia sensed or perhaps had caught a whiff of what I was saying and laughed. We did not want Barkat to hear.

We waited an hour at the Aminuddaula Park, and the procession finally wound its way there. Jingles galore were heard, some of them borrowed from Delhi. '*Gari ka number 88 / Gari pahunchi India Gate / India Gate se aayee awaz / Indira Gandhi zindabad.*' Nirupam Khera whom people had seen riding a ramshackle bicycle only a month earlier was now ensconced in a Jeep. A roar from the crowd greeted him as he climbed on to the stage, festooned with Congress banners, tricolour, spinning wheel and all. He himself was festooned with marigold garlands and a shawl. Suddenly the hubbub died down. 'Friends,' he began, 'today is a day when patriotism has triumphed over treason and nationalism has won against foreign collaborators. We are here to felicitate the saviour of our country and national honour, Indiraji. Shout with me, Vande Mataram! We all remember how she defeated the Pakistanis singlehandedly in Bangladesh. Even Atal Bihari Vajpayee called her "Durga Ma". I wish to speak to you on discipline.' (He pronounced discipline as "dispaleen".)

'Look friends, leadery is no joke. It is a God-given talent. One out of many millions has it, this quality. Indiraji has it from her *sanskar*. What kind of a country are we? You have heard the saying "seven Kanujias, nine cooking fires". Can such a country progress? Six people sit at breakfast; one wants *aloo paratha*, another *methi-ki-roti*, a third wants fried eggs, the fourth demands omelette without onions, another wants omelette with onions and green chilies. You think our Bharat Varsh can progress this way? Mrs Gandhi says only aloo-ka-paratha today, nothing else, and some yogurt. Jolly well eat and be happy! Eat and ismile! Now that is discipline, that is leadery!' The crowd roared in approval. Chest-thumping Youth Congress leaders spoke one by one. We wanted to leave before the meeting was over, but could not just slink off. When the sloganeering started at the end of each speech, we shouted 'Ram Nath Halwai ki jai', 'Nautanki waleh ki jai'. Some of the bystanders who heard us just gawked, some smiled, but sensing the mood Inspector Ambika Singh again came to our aid, herded us back to the car and saw to it that the crowds on the fringe parted to give way to our vehicle.

The Exorcist

One evening as the street lights came on Rabia walked in along with her brother, Barkat. I noticed that Barkat, who loved dressing in jeans was sporting a cap which Shilpa would have termed 'Musalmani', was in salwar kameez. Barkat was just out of his teens and a good five years junior to us. Rabia made sure Elham was not within listening distance and in a low voice told me that people are going to come to your house this evening immediately after the evening namaz. A self-styled Maulvi, Azmatullah from Golaganj was to make his way to our place in Qaiserbagh and demand to take Elham away from me. 'And why is that?' I asked. Before she could answer, we saw about a dozen people at the gate and asked the gardener to open it. We came out in the veranda to confront them. There were three women in the group, including Fauzia. The leader of the group was obviously Azmatullah, dressed in a sherwani with buttons open (it was hot and sticky, a typical late July evening). He came up the veranda steps and stood there, eschewing any greeting or salaam. That is not how Lakhnavis behave. He was fat and had a skull cap on. He had a fleshy face and a goatee under his chin. Fauzia spoke first, saying she had nothing to do with this and had come along only to make it clear where she stood. Azmatullah silenced her, telling her and obviously me, that Fauzia should let him speak. Looking straight at me Maulvi Azmatullah said, 'I am here only because some people of Golaganj have complained about this house'.

'This is Qaiserbagh and not Golaganj. And what is the complaint?'

Before I could add anything, Rabia stepped forward and asked, 'Azmatullah Sahib, who has given you the authority to look into complaints?' Barkat added sarcastically, 'Have you by any chance become an honorary magistrate?' Even one or two men in Azmatullah's group snickered. Azmatullah was not going to let his authority slip away so easily. He had a deep voice and looked very dignified, I must say.

'You are aware Thakurain Seemaji that it is a sin to keep a djinn in the body?'

Holy cow, how was I to answer that. I became tongue-tied. But Rabia said aggressively, 'Say what you have to say.' Our bearded friend snubbed her.

'I am talking to the Thakurain, I want an answer from her.'

It was the first time I had ever been addressed as Thakurain. 'I am not aware what djinn you are talking of and where he has sprung up from, Azmatullah Sahib.'

'I am talking of the djinn in Elham's body, Fauzia Begum's daughter's body. Keeping a djinn in the body is a sin, it is written in the Qoran Sharif, it's as bad as cohabiting with someone.' I looked at Rabia, even she was taken aback. None of us knew what was written in the holy book. He went on, 'And it is specified that there are two types of djinns, Muslim djinns and non-Muslim *(gair Musalman)* ones.' Fortunately Barkat intervened here. 'What about Sikh djinns and Yahudi djinns, Maulvi Sahib? And have the Muslim djinns been circumcized? Or how would you know they are Muslim djinns?'

'I have no time to answer absurd questions, [*fazul ke sawalat*]. I am only competent through Allah's *meher* to eradicate a Muslim djinn.'

Barkat persisted, 'Do you have a certificate?'

'I told you Barkat Mian that I have no time for absurd questions.' It was my turn to ask, 'Azmatullah Sahib, how will you eradicate the djinn?'

'By reading *ayath*s from the Qoran.'

'You will not beat the girl?'

'Allah *kasam*, I won't.'

'How will we know that the djinn has left her body?' I asked, and Barkat followed up by asking, 'Will you *chidko* some *itr* on him so that we know by the smell that the guy has fizzed out.'

But Elham had heard it all. She came out and stood defiantly there and said, 'I will not go to this man or anyone wanting to drive a *bhoot* out of me. There is no one inside me. I am there inside myself.' And she went back in and banged the door.

I have a confession to make, I have never really got into Elham's problems because she comes across as a closed door, I am not trying to deflect my own shortcomings. She must have been very confused with her own visions/hallucinations, call it what you will. I felt incompetent to deal with this psychobabble, and I didn't wish to deflect her from whatever she was up to in this dubious near-occult field of hers. I found myself low on taboo, but also low on empathy. I tried to empathize with her (did I?) but it is not easy to move into another's suffering. Suffering is a palisaded enclosure—it does not always welcome intruders.

Letter in a Bottle

This is not a letter to you alone Mama, it's a letter in a bottle consigned to the sea—the waters of fate, just as babes in all myths were put in a small boat—Moses, Romulus, and Remus. The moment you enter myth you enter hyperbole, the *vahan* that carries you into another world. Back to earth, one needs to speak of the family sometime. Men may be anchored in their land or vocation; women are anchored in the family. So if my letters fall into the hands of a reader, let her or him know a bit about the gene tree. To switch metaphors slightly, I will refrain from landscaping the family vineyard; will just sketch a trellis overlaid with a vine and be done.

As family lore has it, great grandfather was a big zamindar with about fifty villages in his jagir. His polio-stricken elder brother remained single all his life, you couldn't get a decent Rajput bride for someone club-footed who needed two sturdy lower-caste shoulders to lean on for even a trip to the loo—it's another thing that there were no loos those days. Then lightning struck the house. Great grandpa (GGP for short) joined forces with Maulvi Ahmadullah Shah of Faizabad in the great Indian Mutiny of 1857. The maulvi was at Lucknow with 1200 of his armed *murids*, disciples, to take on Major General James Outram. After Waterloo this must have been the most talked about military engagement in nineteenth century British history. (They don't talk too much about their non-exploits in the Crimean War, if you've noticed Mama, but reams have been written on the stoic heroism displayed at the Residency. It was the nineteenth century version of Dunkirk.) The elder brother—so goes family folk lore—was spying for Outram and sent notes to the British garrison through two trusted Baheliyas. Even this could not save GGP from the gallows, but the jagir was only pruned and not taken away.

Ahmadullah Shah had it coming. He escaped the British dragnet for months, despite the Rs 50,000 reward the East India Company announced on his head. Fifty thousand was a hell of a lot those days, not sure if Mir Jaffer, whom Robert Clive bribed, got a larger amount. A reward for a head must have been a metaphor Mama, isn't it? The governor general wouldn't have wanted a gory head with bloody locks deposited on his table. (I have seen a painting in a book Mama of Medusa's severed head, blood all over her dreaded locks. Was it Hercules or Theseus who decapitated her? Never mind.) But one minor Raja Jagannath of Shahjahanpur was not aware of the difference between metaphor and physical fact. He invited Ahmadullah Shah to his fort, and when the unsuspecting maulvi on his elephant came near the fort, Jagannath's brother shot the maulvi dead. He then cut off his head and galloped to the house of the district magistrate of Shahjahanpur, who was having lunch. Spinach soup and fish mayonnaise were just over, fish fork and fish knife removed, rice and curry yet to come, Raja Jaganath barged in with Ahmadullah's severed head and deposited it on the dining table, thus securing his fifty thousand. Doesn't make for good reading, couldn't have made for a good lunch for the DM.

Grandad went to the Colwin Talukdar College. The Brits were keen on the college, for most of the Talukdars had sided with the rebels as they were called. He married a jagirdar's daughter from Bihar.

The life they lived appears in my Mama's journal and I am not going to waste time talking about their lives, the forty acres of rice that he sold to get away from the Brits in India, only to land in Canada. I meant to talk of myself. It was years before the Emergency on a Sunday that I first saw him. My editor asked me if I could attend a seminar at the Secretariat. A seminar in the UP secretariat, I couldn't believe it! Nothing remotely connected with anything intellectual had ever trespassed into these holy precincts. I had nothing much to do at home, so went along. The seminar was on prisons and prison life, something of that sort. The figures trotted out were grim—ratio of under-trial prisoners to convicted criminals, number of years spent in jail when the final outcome was acquittal, women prisoners and their living conditions in jail. Some of them become pregnant there, how come, asked one outraged speaker. Someone read a paper on prison, which was refreshing—it was not all about Nehru and the books he wrote in jail, *The Discovery of India* and the like. He talked about the panoptical jail in the Andamans, and emphasized that it was not all about *kala pani* and depression. All the inmates were not political prisoners, and the criminals among them sometimes sang as they came on boats to the islands. In passing he mentioned Manohar Malgonkar, who had quoted a song in one of his novels, he didn't remember which. And he looked around hoping someone would bail him out. One guy stood up and recited (I quote from memory now):

Bol jawanon kya kya milat hai
Kala pani ke bazar, ho kala pani ke bazar.
Muft ki andi muft ki brundi
Aur muft ki randi hazaar,ho muft ki randi hazaar.

Some in the audience giggled, a few even clapped. What in effect they sang was that in the jail in Andamans they would get free eggs, free brundy (brandy) and a thousand prostitutes(some hope!). Before the speaker could continue with his paper, the guy who had recited the lines, spoke up again, smiling, with a twinkle in his eye, 'Mr Chairman, I'll have you know that I remember these lines because of the rhyme and not because of the randis.' The chairman assured him that he believed Mr Nishant Singh. (That's how I came to know his name.)

'People can harbour all kinds of thoughts, Mr Chairman, so I thought I better clarify.'

There was general merriment at this exchange. I certainly enjoyed it. The girl sitting by my side said, 'How brash!' But her friend immediately laughed, 'What élan!' That restored my confidence in my judgement.

At a buffet lunch, I was a part of a group when he came over and started chatting with me. Well, that's how we met for the first time. Two years later we were married. He belonged to the Indian Administrative Service—the IAS—belonged to Bihar, and was allotted the UP state cadre. He had high connections in Bihar, we were told. During our courtship—he was courting me—I asked him why he wanted to marry me. What did he see in me? Looks, he answered, just one word, you know all that Mama, its déjà vû for you. He hated district life, didn't want any of it and managed to hang on in

Lucknow, to the envy of his compatriots, that is till he moved to Delhi a year or so back. Nishant had got into the Ministry of Mining because it was headed by a Bihari godfather.I had, of course, gone along with him. We got a house in Kidwai Nagar, with Safdarjung Hospital and the All India Institute of Medical Sciences (AIIMS) just across the Ring Road.'I don't know what to do about my job,' I told him. He didn't answer. 'Nishant, I am a serious journalist, don't forget.'

'I know that Seema, and have not forgotten that you topped in your journalism class. I also remember that you did very well in your post-graduation in English. We'd better try our luck at some newspaper on Bahadur Shah Zafar Marg.'

'If anyone tries there Nishant, it will be me alone, not you. I am not going to muscle my way into Delhi journalism via the IAS, if you don't mind. It would ruin my reputation for ever. At the moment, I don't want to leave the *Lucknow Chronicle*. I have my roots there. I will see if I can become their Delhi correspondent.'

He added,'And you also have your book.' Yes, my project on Kangra art. Why I took to it, I wouldn't know. Perhaps because father had left me that 'pad', as Alfie had dubbed it, in Kangra. Mama you used to spend the entire summer there, remember. Then came an exhibition of Kangra paintings to Lucknow. Mama, you presented me that lovely book on the subject by Randhawa. He belonged to the ICS. Why doesn't the civil service produce such people now?

Anyway, my editor at the *Lucknow Chronicle* consented to my working from Delhi. I was soon to find it is the wrong place for a 'budding' journalist. Delhi was all politicking in drawing rooms. The scribe tribe that really thrived here was an assured lot, studied abroad, smoked incessantly, flirted with famous cricketers, were on dear-and-darling terms with cabinet ministers, especially ministers like V.C. Shukla, people who could throw a few French phrases as they blew their cigarette smoke into your face, who could call Indira 'Indi' and cluck their tongues, shake their heads sorrowfully and say 'We must do something for the poor, so glad you are at it Indi', that kind. I may be exaggerating a bit Mama, wouldn't know how many dared call her 'Indi', but what kind of a journalist would I be if I didn't stretch a few things? Journalism is a stretching exercise, keeps the joints trim. They were not above pronouncing sherbet as sorbet, you bet Mama. There were also the anti-socialists, hand-me-downs from the Swatantra party, equally arrogant, equally lofty, who had a different take on most things. Their endless rants would, I am certain, extend into the next century, with nothing falling in the laps of the poor through all these socialist exercises. All that dribbles down to the poor is dirty water, they say.

There are always exceptions even among the lofty ones though. A colleague of Nishant's was blessed with a daughter, and a month later he threw a party, whiskey flowing, Indian of course. If you served scotch those days you were marked as corrupt. I noticed a lady in starched white sitting apart from the rest, a bit older than our crowd, smoking incessantly. I noticed her nicotine-stained fingers, her nail polish resembling aluminium rather than silver, and a similar coloured lipstick. Everyone was congratulating the host with cries of 'Lakshmi has entered your home', 'Lakshmi has crossed the threshold', Lakshmi this and Lakshmi that. The aluminium painted lady had had enough. 'What is all this Lakshmi business? Come on, a daughter is born and that should be cause enough for rejoicing. Why are we linking her arrival with wealth? She is here and we stand blessed. Don't bring Lakshmi into this.' Am not sure whether I liked her outburst more or the stunned silence that followed.

For someone like me with no roots in Delhi, and no claims on either Anand Bhawan or Wardha, things were tough. The moment you approached someone, you were asked where you lived, guy wanted to place you, nail you to the galli, kucha, moholla, palace or pigsty you lived in. I wanted action in the street, that kind of event I had covered, including the decade long stoning between the police and the students at Monkey Bridge in Lucknow. They really chucked the stones hard, the students, or the cops who retaliated could have been a match for some of the bowlers from Serendib, come to think of it. Here getting an accreditation card as a journalist to enter the Parliament (Vigyan Bhavan was not yet built) was a headache, the process endless, filling forms, affixing passport photographs and getting a letter from MLAs or MPs certifying you were a decent girl and not a witch. It was a marathon with no finishing point in sight.

No one 'called' on anyone here, each lived in his or her cubbyhole. Evenings were spent walking up to the INA Market across the road, buying fish, vegetables and fruit. I felt like a bath after a visit there. I had lived a better life in Lucknow. People were less chauvinistic here—they still had a Warren Hastings Road and a Curzon Road. I surely knew what that Hastings fellow had done to our Begums of Avadh. Nights were creepy. With two big hospitals across the Ring Road, the ambulances would scream in. Why the hell did they have to let go their sirens full blast at two or three in the morning when there was no traffic anyway, I have never understood. Nishant was quite happy though. His minister, a Brahmin from Bihar, was very happy with him. He even took him along on his tours, mostly mining areas in Orissa and Bihar. The only time he came back grumpy was when the deputy minister took him along to Dubai of all places. Nishant came back fuming. The minister had unloaded a VCR on him, after purchasing two himself. And they walked through the Green channel. Nishant had also got a mouthful from our consul general, a real Foreign Service type, languid in his walk, and words flowing from his mouth in a waterfall of golden syrup. 'Mr Singh whom does your Deputy Minister expect to meet here? If I might suggest, his expectations should not be pitched too high. They'll give him some Turkish coffee and a plate of dates and praise the Emergency and perhaps present a silver dagger as a gift, which in any case he will have to give back to our Tosha Khana, and that's about it. They never enter into any substantial discussions—it ain't a part of their diplomatic genes, if you get me mate. You had better forewarn him.' Yes I had heard stories of the IFS. I had been told that while the husbands revelled in their waterfall of vowels, things changed if they came back from a trip without the olives from Granada—Lorca country Mama, or marzipan from Amsterdam, and that chiffon sari from Paris. Then the wives let go a consonantal cataract of curses, though one of the wives confided in me that 'asshole' sounded more 'vowelly' than she would have liked. Hope you are enjoying my alliterations Mama, I am turning quite proficient in them, don't you think? But they are quite high class, Mama, these foreign service types—they call themselves 'elitist'—wouldn't be found dead calling themselves 'high class'. And they are high caste—all tendentious Tambrahms and noir Nairs. They won't allow a Jat in unless he is a Kunwar and married in some royal family or the other.

By now you have seen through my lies, you always did. They are as decent or indecent a lot as us. It is language that leads me on to all this. Language is a whore standing on a balcony and soliciting. Come hither with your curses and swear words, also imaginings, fancies. So then what can you do but walk up the stairs? But back to the Dubai trip. Worse followed when the consul general decided to ask the deputy minister, 'Sir, what will be the *sonum bonum* of your Excellency's parlance with the Dubai Excellency?' In other words, 'Minister, what specifically is your brief, Sir?'

'Oh,' said the deputy minister, 'I will ask them to check smuggling goods into India in their dhows!' With some difficulty he and Nishant persuaded the minister to refrain from this line of action.

Things were not equally happy in the country though. Gujarat asked for rice, someone in the PM's Secretariat misread the cable and sent trains full of the Central Reserve Police instead. Jai Prakash Narayan called on the police and the army not to obey illegal orders. Dicey bijness, Netaji. Who is to decide which order is legal? There were calls for total revolution. Who is to decide on the totality or otherwise of a revolution? People were getting confused. But the first I heard of the Emergency was when I opened the newspaper and found an article on how to prepare onion raita on the front page. Hell's bells I said, something has gone wrong with the country. How could the preparation of onion raita assume national importance? I opened the *Indian Express* and it had a blank front page. They are short on printer's ink, was my first fear, the great Ramnath Goenka left printless, high and dry! I phoned Nishant at the office and told him about the raita story, and the *Indian Express* blank page and suggested that papers were running out of printer's ink probably and could he do something about it when he just, to my utter humiliation, shut me up. 'This is no time to crack jokes,' he barked and put the phone down. I rang up Shilpa in Lucknow. 'Leaders are being arrested. Don't talk on the phone! I thought Delhi would drill some sense in you.' Phoned Daksha, she said the same thing, except she was even more rude than Shilpa. Our blunder that morning was we hadn't listened to the news. When Nishant returned around nine in the evening I heard the full story. It seems at midnight while the president was in the bath tub…

What was he doing at midnight in the bath tub, for Chrissake?

Having a bloody bath Seema, what else. Well there was a knock on the bathroom door.

'Who is it?' asked the president.

'Om Mehta, minister of state for home, Sir.'

'What do you want?'

'Sir, you may kindly sign this ordinance.'

'Let me first dry myself,' said the president, 'I mean let me first soap myself, then wash the soap off and then dry myself. You got me confused!'

After seven minutes the door squeaked open, the papers were passed on to him and he signed. When later he was put up before one of the fifty Commissions set up by the Janata government and asked whether he had seen the 'Signing Authority', the minister denied seeing him sign. 'The signatures were affixed in sanitised privacy, your honour,' said his defence lawyer, who held a ME (Master of Euphemism) degree from St Stephens. 'So how would you know the document bore the president's signature? Did you send the document to a handwriting expert before implementing what was in the ordinance, Mr Minister, I mean Mr ex-Minister?' asked the learned judge-chairman of the Commission. Minister had no answer. 'Why didn't the president step out of the bathroom and sign?' 'Your Honour,' said the defence lawyer representing the minister, 'the President had a towel wrapped around him'.

Judge: 'Has the towel been produced in evidence as an exhibit?'

The attorney general sprang to the defence of the prosecution, worried that the Commission was looking for a loophole to acquit the ex-minister of state for home affairs (MHA). 'Your Honour it was too wet to be packaged and sealed.' That mollified the judge a bit, and he wrote in the judgement that the signing in the washroom did not make the ordinance '*actus reus*', meaning a guilty act, because the President was *'compos mentis'*, meaning in full command of his faculties. (The judge was fond of Latin quotes and defence lawyers were usually ready with their own arsenal from Latin limbos. One lawyer was reputed to have bought a bilingual edition of Dante's *Inferno*, hoping to pick up some juicy phrases to impress the judge.) The judge did not forget to note down that in future it is a must for a constitutional authority to be seen while he or she or the transgendered office-and-seal-holder signs a legal document. Signing ceremonies need to be avoided in bathrooms, bedrooms and kitchens, of course all this was said in very legal language, much of it in archaic Latin. Dante would have been pleased—must find out whether he wrote in Latin or Italian. The attorney general bowed, ex-minister shrugged, defence lawyer smirked and the matter rested there.

I forgot to tell you that the minister for state had to barge his way through a horde of chaprasis, guards, trumpeters—the ones who came out with the fanfare—to reach the wash room. He had some para-military with him and a few IB hoods carrying pistols.

At home we had been debating what I should be doing. Nishant thought I should forget my 'hare-brained' (as he termed it) project on Kangra painting. 'Who is going to publish what you write? You are not an acclaimed art critic. People will look for your credentials and not find any. A book on painting without the paintings on glossy paper means nothing. If you go in for a coffee table book, publishers will be even more reluctant. The investment in that kind of thing is considerable. You have to go to publishers in Singapore for good reproductions. The decision is yours. I can't come in the way.' I was adamant, however. I was halfway through with my manuscript and not finishing it was causing me a lot of tension.

He would also get into a jocular mood. 'Why can't you let Sansar Chand rest and start looking at your own *sansar*?' Raja Sansar Chand (1765–1823) was the king who had encouraged Kangra painting. Once Nishant even dared to denigrate this art as 'stylized myth'. What the hell do you mean by that, I barked. 'Look at this one,' he said, picking up a book I had bought on the subject and pointing to a painting. This is Rama and Sita during the fourteen years in exile. The forest looks like a park, a plush glade with lovely trees all around, each leaf distinct and painted in varied shades of green. The three of them seem to be on a picnic, with Rama reclining and putting his head on Sita's lap while Lakshmana sits near his brother's knees. Fourteen years in the forests of those days reduced to this. It is a disservice to Ramji and Sitaji and the privations they must have undergone.I fought tooth and nail.

What are those Renaissance paintings all about? The manger, adoration of the Magi, Calvary—aren't they stylized?

'You don't get my point,' he answered. 'You will exploit the already-exploited.' That really enraged me Mama, to even hint that I was an exploiter. I knew what he liked—huge murals, large paintings from one end of the wall to the other. 'Big is not always best, Nishant. This art, the one I am talking about is not loud nor melodramatic. It has a delicate feminine touch about it, even if the artists were men. It is not big art—I am talking of scale. And it was practised by dedicated artists.'

'Did you say desiccated?' he asked with a silly grin, and walked off.

This was all prior to the presidential signature on the Emergency ordinance. Now things had heated up. I had started railing against the Emergency. I had a few friends for dinner and announced with a flourish that I was serving the Emergency raita, prepared according to the recipe which appeared on the front page in a national newspaper. People giggled but I could also observe the raised eyebrows and the look of fear which gripped the guests.

One day he returned from office and as usual I blasted the Emergency. 'Nishant, there isn't a politician from the opposition who is not in jail. Even the Ranis—I mean Jaipur and Gwalior—are in the cooler. Do you understand what that means? It is total dictatorship. Stalin couldn't have done a better job.'

'Every opposition leader is not in the cooler. The communists are basking in the Emergency sunshine.' He smiled wickedly, knowing my proclivities towards the Left. What the communists were up to was shameful of course, but then they had backed Stalin and even Mao. Nishant was not done. 'And some of the slippery guys are missing.' I got a jolt. 'Missing' could even imply they had been done away with. He reassured me on that and added, 'George Fernandes and Subramanian Swamy have slipped away'. It was the first I had heard of their escape.

'Look Seema, you don't seem to have any idea what I face day in and day out. At the office I point out where the Emergency has been discussed (mostly adversely) in the foreign media. I draft notes and press despatches defending government actions—that's my bloody job. I can't stay on in government and also criticize it—I would be in jail next day and you would have to look for a job as a school teacher or something. Then when I come home I have to listen to your unceasing rant against Mrs Gandhi's dictatorship. Have you ever thought that this kind of conflict or contradiction could be tearing me up inside? Have you ever talked such things over with the wives?' I was stumped. 'IAS wives?' I asked.

'Yes IAS wives, who else?'

'I know what they'd say. How absolutely terrible Seema, imagine we've to live through such days, but what are we to do? As long as kitchen and wardrobe are taken care of, and schooling for children, they have hardly any other concerns. Police wives could be worse. You need some peace, didn't occur to me you could be torn inside, and I could be the cause of it.'

I threw my arms around him, you poor dear, and we went into a clinch—a solid half hour session of kiss-and-cuddle. In the end I said, 'You know me Nishant, I can hardly help myself.' That couldn't have been very reassuring for hubby. Soon I found his resistance to my Kangra adventure getting diluted. Time to strike, I thought. 'Why don't I go away and finish my book?' And that was it, I pushed off to the hills. It's another thing that I could not 'finish' my book.

Peahens and Predators

My kitchen window in Qaiserbagh looks east, and while making my tea I threw it open to let the east wind—the purwaiya—blow in along with the leftover colours of the dawn. The trouble is the east looking window also gets the searing sun. The song playing on the transistor was *Nani teri morni ko mor le gaye/ Baki jo bacha tha kale chor legaye. (*The peacock took away the peahens and dark thieves stole the rest.) The song had a lilt about it and I tapped my way through it and hummed away. What to talk of the peacock, even brown peahens didn't make an appearance on my neglected lawn. But someone from the Qaiserbagh Police Station did. He came in plain clothes with the message that Inspector Ambika Singh wanted to see me, and would drop by at noon. Why does he want to see me, I kept thinking. I wished he came early so that one could finish with this business. Was he coming for Elham, fortunately she was at school. The inspector came an hour earlier, the same guy who had supervised the sterilization camp in the street the other day, the senior guy. He looked different in a blue bush shirt and grey slacks. He never looked overbearing, even in the street that day, unlike his subordinate. I had a glass of cold water served to him and waited till he spoke. He looked around. 'I hope you feel secure.' I nodded saying I had no trouble. Does anyone sleep in the veranda at night, he persisted, and I shook my head. He walked out into the veranda, called out to the gardener Purshotam in a stentorian voice, gave him a needless dressing down and asked him to sleep in the veranda at night 'till madam is here.' He never bothered to ask for my opinion in the matter. Purshotam was almost trembling, as he retraced his steps and stood near the almond tree.

'Ladies staying alone can't afford to be careless. These are bad times.'

'I thought you considered these good times, the way you marshalled the sterilization camp.'

'I was only seeing to the law and order. All this can't last for ever, nasbandi and the whole tamasha. How long can you keep Maharani Jaipur and Gwalior in jail, tell me, how long? *Kab thak chalegi yeh nautanki*?'

I noticed he wasn't so bothered about Jai Prakash Narain (JP) and Charan Singh and Moraji Desai in jail. Maharanis in jail still bothered the man on the street. Was he probing? He switched to asking me about the health of Nishant Singh Sahib. I assured him he was fine. 'He must be worried,' he said. 'I mean with such a responsible job, he must also be needing support.' He stood up to go. 'Take care of your security. Please remain alert. The Special Branch tells us there is too much *hul chul* in the house. And when you go out alone, please don't take rickshaws, take taxis.' Taxis, I told him, cost a lot. He smiled.

'There are two suspects on the Faizabad Road, one of them is a big fish, a crocodile rather, but we don't have the exact location. And Faizabad Road stretches right up to Faizabad.' He smiled again and left. I kept wondering who the crocodile could be in this urban swamp.

That night I dreamt of throwing open my windows to a stiff breeze—it was not the same house, seldom is in dreams—but I was there and I felt the house was mine. Dreams are not just visuals, feelings are part of the play. The breeze was strong and sent the curtains flying. But I was alone in the house, that feeling didn't leave me or the dream—dreams too have a body and a mind somewhere. Which or what is that reality there spinning away at sign and symbol—strong breeze, flying curtains and me alone trying frantically to bring order in the house, or in my life. Who is this psychiatrist on whose loom such dreams are woven? It told me I was alone and my life needed some order. Suddenly, you find that loneliness has nowhere to empty itself except in your dreams. Time to be back with Nishant.

Delhi O' Delhi

You could have come by air, why take a train, said Nishant as he came to pick me up at the New Delhi station. I chose not to reply. We came home in an official car, chauffer driven, and reached our new home on the junction of the Cornwallis and Wellesley roads. Both names were shortly to be changed to Zakir Husain Marg and Subramania Bharati Marg. We had got a ground floor. How come? I had imbibed the not-so-subtle gradations of Indian bureaucracy, all written in stone. These houses were for joint secretaries, inspector generals, major generals—not for deputy secretaries. But then if you are in PMS, the prime minister's own Secretariat, you got your privileges. Across the Wellesley Road were the Pandara Park flats, meant for additional secretaries and the like. Nishant kept looking at me in the car, I said nothing but I did become jubilant at a ground floor Bapa Nagar flat as I got down. He felt happy. It had a lawn and a long veranda looking out into the open, and we were away from the Ring Road (there was no Outer Ring Road then) and there were no ambulance sirens making their staccato sorties into hospitals at night, for there were no hospitals nearby.

I did not get tea ready for him when he came back around eight in the evening, it was no time for tea. Right after a wash he pulled out a bottle of scotch and the Jeeves pulled out a cold soda bottle from the fridge. I noticed the upgradation in whiskey also, in Lucknow he had stuck to Solan and Black Knight. The bottle he had pulled out from the bar was Vat 69, the bar also new, carved—had the new, rich Gujarati stamp on it. He offered me a drink which I declined.

It was after dinner that he unwound and told me what happened at the office, nothing dramatic, drama had actually forsaken the political world. If there's no opposition there is no drama said Nishant. I let him speak, checking my habit of cutting in. I wanted to say there could be drama in the jail, but kept mum. It seems a journalist from Bihar approached a series of his contacts to eventually gain admission into the deputy secretary's hallowed office. It had taken the poor fellow a month to get to Nishant. He showed him his four-page rag that he published every week. Nishant asked him if there was an arrest warrant chasing him. 'No Sir, but police these days are not bothered about warrants. Sir, I never introduce any politics in my paper, there is nothing against Mrs Gandhi or JP or even some unknown MP or MLA. I am just a yellow journalist, Sir.'

I took the car out and was appalled the way they drove here. At every traffic light you heard a cacophony of car horns. If the light was red, they were asking you to plough ahead, never mind the light. If it turned green there was more of honking, asking the guy ahead to move fast so that the bum behind could cross before the light turned red. Cars whizzed by on the left, missing me by inches. The people were rude without even realizing that they were being rude. The only good thing I found on the streets was the absence of betel kiosks, less people with sepia-stained wet lips and fewer stains of sepia on the walls. Also less people with gutka and paan masala.

How long can you keep from politics? Politics is not only the smog in Delhi, that decoction of diesel fumes and lies, it is a shawl and hijab rolled in one; it's the Gayathri Mantra that you chant in the morning, the sunset azaan from a minaret also caught in the smog. During Emergency, the surya namaskar was replaced by a namaste to Mrs G. But Mama, any discussion about politics brought up bad vibes between us. I used to daydream about going as a visitor to Tihar and meeting the Ranis Gwalior and Jaipur. If I had, I'd have touched their feet. That morning all this was churning within me when Nishant asked about Kangra. How did it feel being there? I gave a lengthy discourse. 'Funny how I remember the first day, as I motored in. Remember it was winter, grass yellowing, trees black-barked, a wisp of a ground mist that vanished soon. I was observing the scene, goat tracks scissoring away from the main road, pine needles soggy because of a shower, straggling shrubbery. In the town I remember a dhaba cook slapping dough on an inverted griddle, a shuttered paan kiosk being opened lazily by a Tamboli in his dhoti, a chained Bhotia dog who did not bark at us, meaning driver and me, a goitered hill woman carrying fire wood on her head.'

Nishant did not say anything for a while. Then he opened up, he was very despondent here, alone and almost friendless—when the wife is not with you, one is friendless, never mind the cronies in the club and in your own batch, he said. I answered, what did you think I felt like? Being alone in Kangra is worse than being alone in Delhi. Still I was guarded, didn't want him to feel I was snagged in the slough of despond. (Bunyan, what would literature be without you?) 'What was the worst period?' he asked. I couldn't dissemble. 'The worst, Nishant? I remember the date, 29th April when only Justice Khanna stood up for civil liberties, and the Bhagwatis and Begs let the country down.' He nodded, it was a sad day. He had no particular admiration for Mrs G.

It was Sunday morning and I was looking up the horoscope charts, didn't notice he was observing as I went from one paper to the next. *Sunday Standard* was my favourite—Peter Vidal got things right for me. Another paper said, 'Things hinge on close relationships. If you put a foot out of place, you may be criticised.' I went to Peter Vidal. He was more direct. 'Be careful, you bulls, you are on a down-to-earth path. Tread carefully this week. What appears certain today may be a vague memory tomorrow.' Nishant asked me how I had got ten interested in horoscopes. I had no option but to come out with Elham's prophecy that Mrs G would be in jail next year. Told him the whole story, the Azmatullah intervention included. Imagine tackling an offer to drive out a bhoot from someone's belly. We hear stories from interior villages and tribal areas where people are burnt for black magic, *jadu-tona* as we call it. They'd be appalled at our refusal to Azmatullah Sahib, expert on both Muslim and Kafir djinns. Nishant did not laugh at my joke! In fact, he was disagreeably surprised, not at the utterance of the child and her prophecy, but that I had kept the matter from him for so long. But I've told you the whole thing, Nishant.

'Yes,' he answered, 'but only now, never thought to open your mouth earlier! So the whole of Lucknow knows about this silly chit of a girl and her prophecy, as you call it, except your husband, dash good! We have an inspector general police in charge of the PM's security. Suppose he got wind of it and had asked me if I knew anything about this girl? And when I'd have shown ignorance about her, he would have said but she lives in your house in Lucknow, damn it. How would I have looked? Think about it.'

Men can be unreasonable, Mama.

After the Fall

It would be dreary Mama, to tell you all that happened after her sycophants and psychophants, the ones who disliked her more than they feared her, convinced Mrs G that she would win the election. That's what people say. I think there was the seed of a democrat in her, left behind by years with her father's teaching. And she was a watcher of the entire freedom movement. The IB bumbled and how! No one had the guts to tell her she'd lose or worse, the sleuths didn't know. I had dragged Nishant to the Ram Leela grounds—didn't take much effort, JP is his idol, or was till he died. It was an experience seeing all of them on the stage, from JP and Morarji to Charan Singh and Bahuguna. Jagjiwan Ram was there also. Nishant thought Indira would put up a fight at the hustings, though she'd lose. I ferried voters in our car on the day of polling, one of the great days in Indian history. And as the results came out, people danced in front of the *Hindustan Times* office score board. And I am not going into detail—the fight for the office of the prime minister. Suffice to say the caustic, ascetic Morarji Desai took over. After that how the press and the radio and the TV went to town on excesses of Emergency. Heady stuff.

But life is where home is, Mama. Well, news came that a roof of one of our outhouses had caved in. Rabia phoned and said it would cost at least a thousand. I wanted an excuse to go to Lucknow. He was going to be thrown out any day, after all the entire bureaucracy was being shuffled around. Nishant would be shunted back to the state, probably to Lucknow, of that I was certain. I told him I would see to the repairs and come back, at the most, within a week. I went back to my city.

The outhouse was really in a mess, half a roof caving in. Rabia helped out, got me a repair man and a roofer. Emergency was off and so one had to pay for the cement in the black market, I was told. I flogged my connections, asked Nishant over the phone to contact his colleagues in the service and help out. He wasn't eager at all—hadn't kept in touch (where was the bloody time!) with his UP colleagues—would be embarrassing, he said. Well, face the embarrassment or shell out money which we don't have, I barked over the phone. (The phone bill in Lucknow hadn't been paid and it was a wonder the telephone guys had not cut the line). They weren't helpful, the officers. A district supply officer told me, 'Madam for a special permit you will have to write an application and fill many forms.' I walked off in a huff, but had forgotten my goggles on his table, and as I re-entered I heard him ask his clerk, 'Who eggjactly does she think she is?' I just picked up my shades and walked off quietly.

Later when I returned to Delhi and told this to Nishant, he was dejected rather than enraged. He said, 'I don't wish to say what I feel, don't want you to hear such words.' But when I persisted he said, 'They think I have been reduced from cat's whiskers to dog's *jhant*s. They don't know how wrong they are.'

You come home or your earlier home and find things have changed imperceptibly. You can't put a finger on it, though. I pulled a book out and found things had changed in the book.

I know that sounds weird. A part of the platform wasn't there, not Charbagh Mama, where I got down sleepy-eyed and dream-befogged, not sure if this platform means anything to you, it does to me; the guards were there though they were half-eaten, but who bothers about guards Mama, you know your daughter is feudal even if born of a communist mother—feudalism is genes, a part of ancestry; but I was bloody sorry that the ghost had gone, poor ghost 'unhoused, unanointed', along with his beard 'sable silverd'. Mama, the silver fish had got to the ghost, Hamlet's father's. It was my BA(Hons) book, marked with red and blue pencils. We performed the first act at Isabela Thoburn, I was Bernardo, and the hall lights were switched off for we had a gaslight on the stage—after all, the scene was 'In the dead vast and middle of the night'. I don't know what to do with the book now, just as Bernardo didn't know what to do with the ghost. And when we change guard I ask Francisco, 'Have you had a quiet guard?' and he answers 'not a mouse stirring.'

Yes and that brings me to the other thing, I noticed rat leavings in the house. I thought of dear old Khalil Gibran.

'If there is rat shit in the house;

Verily there is a rat in the house.'

I was not going to sit idle—dusted the rat trap and next morning got the mouse. He knew he was trapped, and never touched the bread crust or the cheese on it. If you are trapped, first thing that goes out of the window is appetite. I felt for him and asked the maali to take the trap far into the wilds and release the fellow. Those who know they are boxed in deserve another chance. It is only those who are unaware of being trapped who don't deserve a thing.

There were other chores. I got the gate repaired, the iron

had rusted, got the maali to bring a welder who added a few bars at the top. The very next morning Mama, a cat had got hold of a pigeon, obviously climbed the gate and eaten the bird fairly close to the veranda. I think it was a message the fates had sent through the feline kill—the cat will get you no matter how high and strong the gate you put up.

Within a day of my landing, the second-in-command of Inspector Ambika Singh came calling, the same fellow who had indulged in filmy dialogue with me, and had later caught me by the wrist after I had slapped the constable. I didn't want to see him but he just sat in the veranda on a cane chair and waited. He kept sitting as I walked up to him and asked what had brought him here. 'Have to ask you a few questions.' Go on, I said.

'This is a serious matter, I must warn you. Please choose your words with care. I am taking down a statement under 161 CrPC.' My temper was fast rising but I kept it in check. 'What is this about? I thought the old case about slapping someone had been filed long ago.'

'You are right. But I will ask the questions. I would like to know from you the whereabouts of accused Shambhu Nath?'

'Shambhu whoooo?'

'Shambhu Nath Pande, the one who owned the hardware shop which we were sealing and which you showed such interest in.'

I was losing my temper. 'I don't know any bloody Shambhu Nath. My interest in the shop which you all were sealing was purely out of curiosity. Why you were sealing and locking up a shop which was already locked.'

'Think and answer and don't act smart. We could have summoned you to the police station and interrogated you. We have converted this case under section 302—murder—you understand?' I didn't.

'He murdered his wife. We are firstly looking for Shambhu Nath and secondly for the woman he was in love with, or why should he kill wife? No one kills his wife if there is no other woman. Think carefully. I am noting down your statement. You look worried, first sign of guilt.'

This was too much. Did he think I was the other woman? I stood up. 'Get out of my house,' I said. 'Out!' He didn't budge. 'Inspector Ambika Singh will soon be coming. You are in deep trouble madam, and this time Nishant Singh Sahib will not be able to pull strings. He will himself be in dock. Emergency is over!'

It got worse when he left and Ambika Singh came in, tall and gaunt as ever, and looking serious. He went over the case, Shambhu Nath's wife had died of burns. What they had to find out was whether it could be an accident. Ambika Singh found broken bangles on the stairs leading to the landing where the body was found. Even as the investigation proceeded, the Emergency warrant was out for him, he was a political opponent with some clout, a diehard Jana Sanghi. Ambika Singh reasoned with me. 'We have found the auto driver who took you to Faizabad Road. He doesn't know your name but we can put you up for an identification parade.' So that was it. I could curse Alfie. The police had not got to the woman in her forties who spoke to me in her Bombay Hindi accent. And did they know his connection to Alfie? I kept a straight face, lied through my teeth, said I had no idea who this Shambhu Nath was, had never seen him (which at least was true). And I was damned if I was taking any help from Nishant. Yet I felt terrible. I had actually carried a package of money for a man who may have murdered his wife so that he could live with a forty-year-old good-looker! Life couldn't have been simpler.

'I know nothing of what you are talking about, Ambika Singhji.'

'So, you will not cooperate with us?'

'I never cooperated then, remember? And I have nothing to give now either.'

'Do you know the whereabouts of Alfred, the reporter for *Christian Science Monitor*?'

'I have no idea, must be in England'.

The interrogation ended there. You can't avoid a filmy backdrop in India. My transistor was playing Begum Akhtar—

Diwana banana hai tho diwana banade
varna kahin taqdeer tamasha na banade.

Yes, one never knew when one could be turned into vaudeville, a joke.

I booked a ticket and came back to Delhi by train. I wouldn't be caught dead going by air—only wives of the corrupt flew. I have fluked upon a metaphor, Mama. In India you fly high mostly if you are corrupt. I told him about the repairs to the outhouse, and put him wise about what my editor had told me, a literary page all to myself in the *Lucknow Chronicle*. But how does one fill a page sitting here? The Delhi literati wouldn't waste a bad poem (they can't write a good one to save their lives) on a Lucknow paper. They will gas at the IIC and talk of Octavio Paz and Ageya and Sartre (they haven't heard of Camus fortunately) and drink rum by the gallon at the bar and end up doing nothing except scratching their privates. Moreover Lucknow was three hundred miles distant, letters were slow and trunk calls expensive. And the Lucknow literati, still in their oriental daze, would go promenading on Hazratganj pretending it was Cannes or the Rialto in Venice with grumpy gondoliers looking on and tourists fixing their binoculars on Murano.

'That outhouse, was it necessary to go all the way to have it repaired? You could have asked Rabia or Shilpa to get it done, and we could have sent a cheque. Simple.'

'Not so simple, they are friends, not caretakers, each with her own problems—Shilpa is involved with Alfie, Rabia doesn't want to marry and the pressure on her is immense, the family comes up with one proposal after another of some lackadaisical, paan-chewing feudal who does nothing and survives on money left behind by ancestors. She doesn't want to enter a tunnel with *talaq* written at the end of it.'

'How much did it cost?'

'Over a thousand.' This offered me a good opening to tell him about some of his cynical colleagues. I also told him that I wanted the house in order, because sometime or the other we'd have to move.'

'Seema I have been meaning to tell you for sometime, but couldn't get a chance. If we move from Delhi, it isn't Lucknow we'll be going to.'

'Then where?'

'Patna.'

So he's had his cadre changed. Am not so dull Mama, the thought came to my mind instantly. 'So your cadre has changed?' He nodded. 'You got it changed since you were with the PM, isn't it?'

'Where would I get a chance like this, don't you understand!'

'And it never crossed your mind that I should be

consulted! We just say goodbye to my state, and I am not asked, as if I don't matter. I went to Lucknow just now to spruce up the house for you. And when did all this happen, this change of cadre?'

'Just forget it.'

We weren't shunted to Patna or Bhagalpur—he had not spent five years in Delhi and the best thing about Delhi is there are strings hanging like aerial roots from a Banyan tree, you just have to get hold of one. Then your benefactor and you have to wriggle past rules—panels, cooling off period—quote precedents of earlier wrong doings (which you get from DOPT, that's Department of Personnel and Training) and you get through. Nishant had the Bihari lobby behind him. Nothing to worry.

Yet I had plenty to worry, would get distraught each time I thought of the Shambu Nath episode. I had actually passed money to a murderer, or at least an alleged murderer. So what if I didn't know he was a murderer. And someone who had killed his wife, if that Ambika Singh was to be believed! Thought of twisting the phrase, how about 'carrying kerosene to wife-burner'. There was a saving grace—this guy had done it for love or lust, not for dowry. Don't know what you'd have said Mama, you would have probably reached for a stick. And there's always the intriguing possibility that he is innocent.

Meanwhile I got hold of a seedy room in Amar Colony and opened an 'office'. The *Lucknow Chronicle* sat cheek by jowl with the Amar Colony Post office. One had to go about twenty steps down from the road to reach it. The Krishna Consciousness Temple was coming up half a mile away and it was spreading and spreading. Word soon got around we were looking for poems and stories and amazingly people started trooping in.

Chatrapati Aurangzeb

There were six of us and we were drinking away at the bar. I was nursing my hot coffee. You should know a little about my friends in Delhi, Mama. There's Daksha of course, she shifted from Lucknow quite some time back, and has sobered down after marrying Daya Shankar, a Mathur who has excised his caste name. But he lives in Mathur Lane alright. It branches off from Curzon Road. Caste names are a bit of a cross now, you get saddled with all sorts of things your caste has been guilty of, from burning your widows on the pyre to flaying hides. There was Sunil Mahajan, a journalist who had once worked with *Thought* magazine, who was jailed by the lieutenant governor and his secretary (people took their orders from the secretary who had a direct line to Mrs G's house). Anyone associated with anything to do with *Thought* magazine had to be a suspect. Thought and tyranny never go hand in hand, Mama.

But friends can wait, it's getting to be a long list. You want to hear about our quasi 'literary' evenings and some of my escapades in Delhi? Well, take this one. It was at the Press Club—seedy building, seedy waiters, seedy pressmen Mama, though now they were glorying in their new found freedom—you'd think they had got rid of Mrs G rather than the North Indian voter. The Southies are still leaning towards Mrs G—how they love a mother figure Mama, as if the whole peninsula was raised by step-moms. The pressmen were almost strutting around at their newly won freedom though during the Emergency some of them were as quiet as my trapped mouse who wouldn't touch the bread splinter and the cheese. The press would not have given up on the cheese though. We were at the Press Club because a Bajpai lady from the South Asian Studies, Stanford was giving a talk on 'British India and Constitutionalism'. Why in the Press Club, I had wondered. Her talk centred on the problems facing the British. Who exactly was the Indian, Hindu, Muslim, Tribal, Untouchable? She started with the reforms of Morley and Minto of 1909 which instituted separate Muslim electorates for the first time. They saw India through the prism of group identities, and cared for the groups and she traced this history right up to 1935. What riled the audience was she never once attacked the Brits on 'divide and rule', the favourite ploy of our politicians. The Brits did this to us, otherwise we were brothers, in 1857 we were united. Muslims gave up eating beef! She had to hold up her hand and say, 'Please listen before you holler me down.'

Afterwards we sat around, Sunil Mahajan, Daksha and her husband and I. We ordered a drink or two. A few youngsters from the press joined us. We started, as such gatherings start, you could draw a parallel with an Indian classical vocalist—tentative tapping on the tabla, the vocalist gargling with word and raga to begin with, testing mike and larynx. A guy from the press complained about the traffic. I knew we were in for a long plaintive talk by Daksha, she hadn't reconciled to the way the Delhiwalahs drive. Right enough she pitched in. 'Firstly, before I talk of traffic,let us look at Delhi,' she said. Everyone from car mechanic to rickshaw puller is into politics. So the Delhi denizen is *homo politicanus*. Half of Delhi is from Punjab; deracinated guys, uprooted, if you don't know the meaning of the word, guys from Gujranwala or Dera Ismail Khan or Dera Ghazikhan. Well, so we can call him '*homo deranicus*'. But when the Delhiwalah on the steering wheel has three whiskies in his belly (Daksha was on her second) and his mistress or his whore sitting to his left, he becomes '*homo satanicus*'! On cue, I applauded vociferously! But there was trouble. A reporter from Karol Bagh hailed from Dera Ismail khan and he almost waded into Daksha. What had made his temper rise to boiling point was that he had been given a flat beer Mama, with no 'beaded bubbles winking at the brim', though he had chewed paan and so was blessed with a 'purple stained mouth'. We got him a good beer, which would have fizzed its way all through Panchkuyan Road, and he cooled down. Daksha escaped unscathed, which couldn't be said of me.

After the traffic snarl there was a sudden diminuendo, happens all of a sudden when the conversation dies. It was then that Dattatray Masurkar, an MP from Maharashtra—Nagpur to be precise—came in. The talk by now had drifted to Delhi politics—Desai, Charan Singh, Chandra Shekhar, Raj Narain and, of course, the Shah Commission. Goings on in the Commission deserved a column in every newspaper on a daily basis. Busy reporters hired brief-less lawyers (they could be had dime a dozen at Tees Hazari or Patiala House) to report on the goings on. We were still in post-Emergency ferment. Even the dead Nagarwala, the chap who is said to have imitated Mrs Gandhi's voice and made the bank manager of the State Bank of India disgorge sixty lakh rupees, had a commission to look into his alleged bungle and death or murder in the jail. First rate raw material for fiction Mama, am certain it will be taken up by some second rate novelist one day. Anyway while we were into all this Mr Masurkar who was sitting quietly so far with a glass full of neat rum, no water, just red rum, suddenly woke up to our conversation.

'Why are you talking of pygmies?' he said.

'Pygmies?' asked Mahajan. 'Sir, we are discussing prime ministers and ex-prime ministers, the one who put half the country in jail.'

Daksha piped in, 'Sir, were you in or out?'

'What do you mean in and out, we weren't discussing cricket to the best of my knowledge.' Some journalists giggled at the MP's sarcasm. I tried to explain, 'What she is asking is were you in jail during the Emergency?'

'I was. But I don't wear that as a badge of honour. It is not like going to jail when we were fighting for freedom.' Indian journalists, however, are a cussed lot. Mahajan asked deadpan, 'And did your party ever lift a finger for freedom, Sir?' A freezing silence followed. Some of us didn't know where to look.

'I mentioned pygmies, because I was thinking of our great men of the past.' How diplomatic to ignore Mahajan.

'Such as?' This time it was Daksha.

'Why Shivaji Maharaj, Chhatrapati Shivaji.' We all nodded. 'We need to get things done.'

'Sir, what exactly do you want done?'

'Raise a statue for him in Matheran or Rajgarh, or some place in the Ghats.' We asked, 'Sir, how many people go to Matheran? The place is a one horse town, you can't even motor down there, not allowed. And, who goes to Rajgarh?'

'People will go there once you attract them, but I won't demean the project I am talking about by calling it tourist traffic. People will go there out of reverence. He was BIG, fought against the Moghuls, was chivalrous towards women, and was at last enthroned as Chatrapati. And don't forget his personal valour. Can we think of a greater man? I want an airport named after him, a Chatrapati Shivaji Airport, or a railway station, something big which the world can see and observe.' (By now he had forgotten Rajgarh and Matheran.)

I piped in now, spur-of-the-moment thought. 'What about Chatrapati Aurangzeb?'

Mama, you should have heard the silence drop like a metal paper weight on a library floor. Yes, silence had come down with a bang. People started looking at each other—that is after they had gasped and grasped what I had said. When you are stunned, your gasping ability comes to the fore but the grasping ability becomes torpid for a moment. Then pandemonium. The Pandies were back, guns blazing, never mind the cow fat in the cartridge, not forgetting the pig fat. Each mouth had turned into a Vesuvius, hot lava spouted from furred tongue through crooked teeth. I only remember the MP, was riveted to his imposing figure.

'Chee chee,' said the MP.

What is so chee chee about it? 'Why he ruled almost the whole country, even the Deccan. And Shivaji went to the Moghul court, remember?'

'Chee chee,' said the MP again, 'you ought to be ashamed of yourself.' And he drew his shawl around him, like Caesar 'muffling up his cloak' after he had been stabbed by Brutus, and walked out. My friends surrounded me and herded me out, lest some of the pressmen beat me up. Pressmen may not be good with words, but some of them sure can use their fists.

Editorial Perils

Mama, much as I skirted the potholes in editing the literary pages of the *Lucknow Chronicle*, I did get into trouble. Actually, if you come to think of it, trouble and I are soulmates. It started off quite well, I mean my literary page. People didn't mind reviewing books. There was this girl who wanted to review *Haveli*. It had won an award. By all means, I said. Since we couldn't pay much, free books were an attraction in our tight-belted, tight-arsed socialist economy. Literary academies in Delhi were willing to part with their award-winning books by non-literary authors for reviews. And there were poems, there always are. The good thing (the only good thing) about poets is they are willing to pay the editor money to see their badly rhymed and atrociously scanned poems in print. Why just the editor, they'd pay the readers if they could get to them. I even came across a moderately plagiarised poem but never wrote back to the 'author'. If I had been dishonest, I could have made a living off poets. She had just pinched four lines and had refrained from using the forklift. I gave her marks for that and kept quiet. Between you and me Mama, if someone can't write, what can she do but plagiarize—there ain't no other option, avenue, casement through the cul-de sac—I had to think hard to get that one right Mama, the stupid alliteration I mean.

Then politics entered my innocent domain, politics or hyper imagination. He was from Sunam or Sangrur or some place bordering Pakistan, and he came up with his semi smutty story about Dera chiefs. Mama, what the Southies who live beyond the Godavari call '*Maths*', the Punjab-Haryana types call 'Deras'. These Deras are governed by semi-Godmen and accomplished lordmen, by which I mean these wannabe holy autocrats rule over their disciples like lords over serfs. I said no to the story. Look at the way it starts. A Dera chief, a bit high on hash, gets up late and finds a reporter who asks him what he thinks of a rival Dera chief. I don't care for him, says the bhang-battered overlord. Don't care for him, says the bewildered reporter, Sir, Guruji, he is said to have cured a lame woman from Mewat who had hobbled upto him and fell at his feet. He lifted her up, placed his hand over her head, closed his eyes and mumbled a mantra. Then he said to her, 'Walk'. And she walked, no wobble or hobble. The hash induced holy one laughed. 'And there will be ten barren women who will vouch for it that he gave them a kid, ha ha.'

The reporter was scandalized. 'Bhagwan, he has half the state cabinet as his followers.' But our man, still sleepy-eyed, waiting for a disciple to bring a neem twig on a silver tray to brush his teeth, picked up a pencil and said, 'He can sit on this and whistle.' Unbeknown to him, the reporter had a video camera in his shirt pocket and an audio hidden in his underwear, and all that the unsuspecting Dera chief had said had been recorded. Then starts the story.

I pleaded my inability to publish this, said no about six times, gave him a cup of coffee, and when he still wouldn't leave, I opened the door, stood there and bade him a respectful goodbye, with hands folded. He caught the hint and left, very sharp, these Dera storywalahs. That is not the end of the story, Mama. In fact, it is the start.

He went to Lucknow and met my editor. The editor, Mr Nigam, didn't like it—I mean what I had done. He hated Dera chiefs, one of them had tried to 'play' with his wife! He bashed me on the phone. Publish it, he said, how else will our *Chronicle* get known? It was published.

That was not the end of the story. First, there were letters from various Dera Chiefs asking if they had been targeted. The secretaries wrote, a Dera chief from Haryana or Punjab wouldn't demean himself writing to an editor. 'I am directed by Bhagwan Shri Shri Shri Dharmraj so- and- so-Anand to enquire if the story published in your rag was directed against Dharmraj and Guruji Mahrajji…so and so.' Such were the letters. Later one of them asked for a written apology. We, meaning my editor and I, asked them to sit on a sharp pencil and whistle. Then they went to the Home Ministry. We soon found these Deras were vote reservoirs. One word from the saffron-robed, sandal paste-smeared holy boss meant a few thousand votes pouring in through sluice gates. Sundry ministers made their unhappiness known to us. No playing around with holy men said the Jana Sangh MP—secularism is fine but holiness is finer. You can't evaluate the texture of the sacred, Shrimati Editor. Journalism and profanity have no texture, said an irate politician from Nagpur, the same Masurkar who had rubbed shoulders with us at the Press Club. If you can laugh at them today, you may satirize one of our saints from Hardwar or Rishikesh tomorrow, or hell's bells one of our black capped navel-saluting saints from Nagpur! Seemaji there has to be a *seema*, limit to some things. Sigh.

The editor shrugged off everything and left it to me to

handle. His staple line, I am told was, why come to me? We print blindly what Seema Singh, editor, literary pages, sends us. I don't even look at what she sends, she is so sensible. Don't know what happened to her this time. We shall publish an apology and sack, I mean blacklist, the correspondent who trapped the Dera saint into making that statement. But destiny and Dera goons joined hands, the fates and fat disciples, male furies Mama, the Eumenides disguised as *sadda* (our) Punjab-and-Haryana MCPs. The Dera goons pounced on him and tore his shirt. One of them wanted to strangle him with his own neck tie, can you imagine? They shouted, the Dera chief had never said a word about the other Dera chief—the goons from both Deras were there pummelling poor Mr Nigam. They later printed leaflets branding the tapes as 'a concocted decoction of the yellow kind'. Editor retracted, goons left leaving broken window panes, smashed crockery and mashed neck tie. All's well that ends well. More poets flocked to me, learning that I was truly the boss. You never know when luck smiles on you. A Sankara Tiwari came in one day and said here's my poem. There were just two lines on a blank sheet, with a title:

'Address to the Gods'
Revered hippopotami
Can you tell me what am I?

I looked for the rest of the poem, couldn't find it, and so asked Tiwariji where it was. 'That's the entire poem,' he answered, a bit affronted. 'Someone with the meanest intelligence could have known that this was the entire poem, two masterly lines on identity.' I nodded, 'Please leave it with me, Tripathiji.'

'I am not Tripathi, I am Tiwari!' and he walked off in high dudgeon.

Another story I handled was about a break up of a love affair. And when the lady from Sunam confronts the bounder from Sangrur who had ditched her and got suddenly engaged to her boss's daughter, she said, 'I had no idea *jee* that you were such a bloody bastard, jee.'

A month later, a long-haired boy (so I thought him to be) came in to see me. He was a bit shy but when after half an hour of chit chat I asked him if he was studying for graduation, he told me, he taught in a college in Haryana and was twenty-five years old. I took a deep breath trying not to show my surprise. He talked of this and that, bright fellow, well read. His name was Martin. I refrained from asking where he taught. He left after half an hour of stimulating talk. He had mentioned a philosopher Karl Jaspers, of whom I had never heard. A fortnight later, he came again. Once again we chatted about this and that, mostly about what he was reading. He was reading Schopenhauer. Sensitive boy (don't know why I still thought of him a boy), full lipped (now why the hell did I mention lips?), reading this bleak philosopher, didn't make me feel happy. Then I finally asked him if he wrote. The question rendered him speechless. This can happen to sensitive people. I had noticed he smiled a lot but his talk was pretty pessimistic.

'You shouldn't be reading Schopenhauer,' I told him. 'He will turn you bleaker than you are.'

'Am I that bleak?' he asked. 'Does it show?'

'From a mile,' I told him.

He smiled—that had become a habit with him—a stock response, self-effacing smile. I couldn't compare him to a boxer, glove up guarding the face. He picked up his bag, a cotton jhola which was much patronized by the pseudo avant-garde in Delhi and as he was sauntering out I asked, 'You didn't tell me if you write.' That fairly stopped him in his tracks, as cheap detective novels put it a page or so before the climactic shootout. 'Is it there in the bag?' I persisted. He nodded. 'Let me see it. Story?' He nodded again, surprised I had zeroed in.

As he handed me the story he said a bit hesitantly (actually hesitation was a part of his personality). 'This is a Bardo story—a bit tough to grasp on first reading. You may have to read the book before you get down to the story.'

'This is a story out of Bardo Thodol?' I asked incredulously. He nodded shyly. 'So its Schopenhauer on one side and the Tibetan Book of the Dead on the other, is it?' He didn't answer, and I noticed an odd gleam in his eyes that smacked of defiance, which seemed to say, you caught me there, but so what? I stand by it. The self-effacing manner had left him. There's metal in the fellow, I thought to myself.

'Can I read the story in your presence?'

He shook his head and almost bolted out of the door. Funny guy, I shook my head. Who is going to read a story out of the Bardo? My readers will think I am mad. So will the editor. But I had nothing better to do, so I rummaged through the pages he had left with me. I glanced at the top of the page and found the story entitled 'The Third Day'. Then I glanced at the bottom of the first page with dismay—dotted with footnotes as it was, looking like a scrawl of dead ants. The story started with a *hpho-bo,* the extractor of consciousness, priestly guy. Tibetans believe that the planet is still with you for at least three days after you die unless you call the hpho-bo, who extracts your consciousness, love and hate, and your memory of near ones and your surroundings. The first thing he does is to drive out the lamentation—that means not just the mourners who have to leave the room but also all grief. The departed has to come to terms with his other existence now. The change is more drastic than say a bureaucrat on transfer finding himself in another office. But the priest of the story fumbles, he's not confident he has dropped his hook into the remnants of the consciousness of the dead guy. I felt a bit creepy reading it Mama, and feel creepy writing about it! He is weighed down with responsibility—these hpho-bo people take themselves seriously. If the dead man's karma permits, will he manage it to the Western paradise of Amitabha? He hopes no one will put that question to him for he wouldn't be able to answer it. Then he plucks out some hair from the corpse, and if it doesn't twitch, the priest has done his job. But the corpse twitches. Mama, after this I got the heebie jeebies, as they say, and left the story a bit tremblingly, if I may say so in bad English. It is like watching a horror movie—doors squealing away, the sudden fall of a brick, a sudden shadow—every jolt has to be sudden, otherwise you might as well go and see *Awara*.

A week later he knocked timidly as he always did, and came in. He looked nervous, but he always did. I read your story, I said. I was of course not going to publish it, so I tried to steer him off course, if I may say so. 'You know Martin, I would have changed an incident or two in the story.' 'Like what?' he asked. 'Well, instead of the corpse twitching when the hpho-bo or whatever plucks the hair of the corpse, I would suggest an alternative.'

'Like what?' he asked again, a bit dazed.

'Well, the corpse could suddenly break into Punjabi, would frighten the life out of the "consciousness extractor", don't you think? Or the corpse could break into singing Heer? What do you think? You could even have two corpses there

Martin. The hpho-bo, could die of shock. The story would gather pace, if I may say so.'

I thought I was brilliant. He thought I was stupid. 'You can't do that, can't play around with Bardo, you're angering the spirits, death spirits, you are in a soup already, just thinking those, if I may say so, absurd thoughts. You are in the realm of the occult, you're not supposed to laugh or turn this into a joke. They may take revenge on me now, or...' he stopped.

Go on, I said, tell me what you wanted to say. He just shook his head. 'Were you going to say that they could even take revenge on me,' I asked. He just nodded, almost shamefacedly, as if apologizing for the thought.

'Now don't publish it,' he said. 'It has been contaminated.'

'Martin, I am upfront with everyone. I was never going to publish it, it's too, how shall I put it, off-beat for the kind of readers we have in and around Lucknow, far too esoteric.' Then I added needlessly—could kick myself—'far too exotic, Martin.' He reprimanded me. 'Exotic and esoteric seem to mean almost the same thing to you. They are poles apart, as editor you should know. And never play around with the esoteric.' He paused a bit, and then asked, looking me straight in the eye, 'Are you one of those who would laugh at a flying Lama, if they saw one—though you would never be given the chance of such an epiphany. You would laugh even hearing about it, wouldn't you? You would jeer at the great Lobsang Rampa himself, isn't it?'

Seeing how tense he was, I did my best to disabuse him of his notions. 'Martin, UFOs and Flying Lamas are fine with me, it is just the corpses twitching away on the third day after they have kicked the bucket that give me the creeps.' Of course I felt queasy lying to him, but I was in no mood to take liberties with the Bardo types. He, of course, was on a trip of his own, hardly listening to what I had to say. 'Madam, they fly, those Lamas, if not physically, then they certainly fly mentally. I am making no sense to you, am I? Well, what I mean is, they fix their mind on something a hundred miles away, and they see everything, as if someone on an aircraft were photographing the place with a camera. He will be able to see the Hans despoiling a monastery, the place savaged, the chronicles scattered to the winds, butter lamps over turned. See what I mean?'

I saw.

Have you anything else I asked. Yes, a poem, he said and left this with me. How bleak, I thought—he's thinking of the end of the universe. Isn't that suicidal in a way? And the manuscript going nowhere except into a state of nonexistence.

Universe as Manuscript

The universe is a manuscript in progress
typed out by an unknown force
[power can never be known or revealed
revelation is a let down, it sheds skin, power and lustre].
Keys keep clacking, universe starts cracking
as it rolls down the typewriter's roller,
lurching and sliding down it's black cylindrical spool.
Impressionists want to get to it with their paints
and impressions, but Mr Typewriter has no sense of colour.

The solar system goes down the spool, also great stars,
Reluctant Aldebaran has to wiggle its buttocks
as it pivots over the roller: flood-waters of light
moving down an escarpment.

Even philosophic tracts roll down, though the
machine is indifferent to both the
imagined Lord's words and those of real heretics.
Ecclesiasts try reading the Lord's prayer
to the machine, some even try hypnosis

and tell the damn Clacketty Clack
that however abstract the Lord may be
the heretics have to be grounded
along with their heresies,
they have a stake on the stake for Chrissake!
Mr Olivetti, please burn this theological stubble.

Light years too roll down the spool, soundless,
and Time gets worried—it will be Time's turn next(!)
The typewriter has no sense-field or brain; bereft of
slogans, binaries, conflicts, griping.
Time and the end of the universe are just defined
by the clacketty clack of the typing.

❁

Wasn't this a good one on meaninglessness, I thought. The universe going down and the brainless typewriter typing away unaware of the great tragedy, the enormity of the process, looked good, I thought. Wasn't it also a metaphor for the fates of Greek myth grinding away exceedingly fine but on the bloody typing machine? And I loved Aldebaran wiggling his buttocks and the flood-waters of light that followed. I cut out that needless line, the heretics having a stake on the stake—no one would understand it, we in civilized India don't burn heretics, we just beat them to pulp—especially the Dera heretics, disillusioned disciples of the godman, who have seen through him. Wish he had left me with a phone number, needed his bio. Never trust these long-haired boys, I said to no one in particular. Would the Lucknavis ganjing along—that's what we called sauntering through Hazrat Ganj—chewing betel and smoking and spitting sepia and *supari* through red lips, and quoting a couplet from Mir or Zauq, take to this Olivetti clacking away and swallowing the universe?

Right then, Daksha came in. 'What have I done, Daksha that you have to look at me like that?' She made an effort to read it again.

'Is this a joke?'

'Not that I know of, Daksha.'

'You can't be serious, printing this kind of thing. Seema, are you going to chamkaofy this?' Since coming to Delhi she had started chatting this way. 'Don't *afsos* karo' and that kind of talk which I didn't take to. You either speak Hindustani or English, no hybrids for me.

'No Daksha, I am not going to burnish this. Would be unethical. Editors are not allowed to do all that.' She looked hard at me, said nothing for a while, and then asked, 'How long do you think you'll hold this job? It does pay you?'

A few days after the issue hit the stands I got my comeuppance. Mr Nigam, the editor, read out over the phone some letters he had received from irate readers. 'Is poetry coming to this, the universe going down a typewriter?' said one. Another said, 'Editor and poet seem to have mistaken objects—stars and planets—for words. Or are they under this poet's spell?' There were dirtier ones—'Is this poet the lady editor's boyfriend?' The Hindi letters were a bit more explicit—they always are. One of them asked: 'Which donkey from which dhobi ghat calls this a poem?' That was civilized, in comparison. I am unable to quote the explicit ones which talked of the possibility of the poet sleeping with me, first time I found Hindiwalahs rather adept at using the F-word. It left me pondering on the phonetic equivalences between the Roman 'f' and the Hindi 'pha'.

The story doesn't end here. Do stories ever end? Aren't they like radio signals in science fiction, beeping away between planets for good? A week later a woman came in, faded sari, large eyes, long tresses. There were no wrinkles on her face though obviously she was in her mid-fifties or thereabouts. Where had I seen her? She would not sit down. A little hesitantly she asked, 'I believe Martin came to see you'. Of course, she had Martin's looks, or Martin had hers. 'Are you his mother?' I asked. She nodded. Then she told me Martin had not returned home since ten days or so. That would date back to our last meeting when I turned down the Bardo story. She sat down and listened to whatever I had to say. As she was leaving I hinted at my misgivings. She asked me to be frank.

'I suspect, without any evidence, that he has suicidal tendencies.' I told her about the story, also the poem. 'Go to the police. Please don't delay.' She nodded and left. The next evening she called and told me she had found a note under his pillow. You are right, she sobbed. The police had looked everywhere but he had left no trace. Ask them to look near the railway tracks, I said on impulse.

This story does end here. The police found him near the rail tracks near the Nizamuddin station, alive, a bit drugged and distraught, but in one piece and pondering suicide.

Of Family

There has to be more to a family than just your name Mama. I am putting things down so that the family history becomes clearer to me, romantic angles, tantrums, shenanigans and the coordinates of relationships. I remember as a child I was confused between the maternal granny and the paternal one. Mama you never wanted to marry, your brother told me, Balbir Uncle. Two names can give a chap schizophrenia Mama, he may start wondering who he is, isn't it? I put this question to your brother and he said 'Don't be a fool.' Late in my teens I had gone to his apple orchard in Kangra, that's where he told me you never wanted to marry, until you got married, that is. He also hinted that you were into calf love with someone older than you and 'above' your station—his words Mama, for me no one is 'above' you. I asked him how he knew all this since he was full ten years younger than you, he said he had heard your Dad, that is Grandpa Thakur Brajbir Singh, telling you off. He was feigning sleep in an adjoining room, Balbir Uncle, and he heard your father say, 'You fell in love and it is over. Now lift yourself and move on.'

Your mother had no idea that you had 'fallen' in love. (I don't even know why people 'fall' in love, why can't they long jump or pole vault into love?) When she heard this, the colour left her cheeks and she fainted. Balbir was told to rush and bring a glass of water as also some cologne from Dadi's dressing table to revive her. The Thakur splashed half the cologne bottle on her forehead and she came to. You were so frightened that you said to her, 'Mama, I have never been in love, I swear. These are just stories that Papa believes.' Granma next day came out with a tirade against her husband. 'See, this is what comes from coming to a foreign country. You can't raise children as you want them to, not in a foreign country of half-naked *mems*.'

Balbir Uncle, since he was born in Canada, had no problems, settling down there a few years after you all left Mexico. He also told me that your father shifted to California a few years after the war ended and the American police was no longer interested in 'Indian revolutionaries'. In California he bought a farm, his first love. Harnam Singh's brother helped him in getting it. I was told you proclaimed from the rooftops you wouldn't marry. You were the one person in the family to come back to India—and you joined the Communist Party. Was also told that you were arrested once and came out of jail only after the case was dropped. The British believed that Congress with its mass following was a bigger threat, though the commies were a vicious lot. Then one fine day you suddenly married father, ten years older than you and a mild, though committed, socialist.

Balbir Uncle found Canada too cold in the winters and came to his apple orchard. I went to him again. I trusted him to be more sympathetic than you, I don't know why. I didn't dare to tell you that I was going steady with Nishant, for your health was cracking, a case of spine TB, according to the doctors. Balbir uncle said what are you afraid of? Tell her, she won't die of shock, let me tell you. She has withstood worse assaults. The boy is a Thakur from Bihar and is a member of the IAS. What more can she ask for? I could break the news to her but she will resent the fact that her daughter did not tell her, trust her with the news.

He also told me about your dad. He could never forget his forty acres of rice land which he had sold to his step brother at almost half the price—the brother had sensed that it was a distress sale for the big Thakur wanted out. The pull of ancestral land is something a farmer or land owner can never resist. It becomes a part of him. He wanted the same acres back and the brother refused even twice the going market rate. He told Kaushalya granny that the brother probably wanted to milk him—he must be wanting four times the price. Granny told him 'Why can't you believe that he is now as much in love with the land as you are. After all, you are the same blood. Just forget about the land.' Thakur Sahib was not convinced. 'I took a round of the land, Kaushalya. None of the old farm workers were there but their children recognized me and did obeisance. Do you understand?'

She replied, 'I understand but there will be no fighting in the family.' Later she asked sarcastically, 'Didn't you hear any *shehnai*s wailing from the Naubat Khana and the drums beating?' That silenced father or so we thought, Balbir Uncle continued. 'The Thakur bought large tracts of land in Rudauli. He even got a red brick Naubat Khana built there, dome and all, and had actual *naubat* players beating their drums. Such is the pull of younger days. What was mine has to be mine again, or at worst, a replica of what was mine.' Balbir Uncle had turned philosophic at the end of the narration.

Mama, of your days in Bombay and Calcutta I haven't

been able to glean much. Balbir couldn't tell me, didn't want to perhaps, apart from saying that it was your father who financed you. Balbir Uncle's analysis was that Thakur Brajbir Singh was stricken with 'philosophic schizophrenia'—his phrase Ma, I wouldn't be caught dead saying things like that. 'What do you mean?' I asked him. He answered, 'Look at his trajectory: landowner, burning-to-be fighter for freedom—it's another thing that he never fought—a bit communist later, I think he absorbed communism through a process of osmosis, interacting with his daughter, your mother. But he was making some money all the time, sawmill in Vancouver, shop in Mexico and then a farm in California. And what happens to his hate for the British—they had hanged one of his ancestors after all, his grandfather if you please. And you've been able to do nothing, you haven't shot, leave alone a Dyer, even a British sergeant or an oppressive indigo planter. Udham Singh and others may have shot the wrong Dyers, if not the General of Jalianwala Bagh, at least the collector with the same name, *ki farak painda hai yaar?*'

Father could do nothing, his circumstances were such. And all this while, which means for the better part of his life he kept up with the news—Easter rebellion in Dublin, Gandhi in Champaran and the Bolsheviks who turned out so bad and bloody that all idealism about revolutions got fucked up—sorry shouldn't use such words in front of you, don't tell your mom.

Doers break through the wall of circumstance, father couldn't. He just kept burning within like an old Hamam in the hills where you keep throwing pine cones and wood shavings into the damned thing and the water keeps boiling and the steam goes up in the air eternally. He had to look after family and finance and an exceptionally talented and beautiful daughter, a linguist who could pick up languages like a magnet picks up iron filings. You've got your mother's looks, her long hair and almond eyes, don't know where the almond eyes came from—we don't have a Mongol or Uzbek in our family tree. But you are a drifter, better to be blunt, have done nothing with languages, a bit of a waster you, that's what I think of you, best to be blunt. (He repeated this damned 'best to be blunt' twice, Mama! Is that a way to disguise cruelty?) So, you understand the philosophic schizophrenia I was talking about? And whatever he may have said he needs must have regretted coming away from California—back to caste and mosquitoes and malaria, a corrupt *patwari* here or a *tahsildar* there and the Englishmen living in an empyrean all their own, with Indian servants eager to pull off the riding boots of sahibs as they return from the paddocks or pig-sticking. British India was Baksheesh India—the third division graduate awaiting clerky as we call it, a lower division clerk's post; the LDC awaiting the baksheesh—how grateful the sod is—for the post of a UDC. And how fair the goras were—no *biradari*, village association, caste politics—Kayastha helping Kayastha, Brahmin helping Brahmin, especially if you are from the same *gotra*; a Sarju Parin Brahmin ain't going to help you even if you are a Brahmin with a plume of hair sprouting from your cranium, in case you are born on the other side of the Sarju river. Now the Hindiwalahs have started calling it Saryu. Sorry pal, wish your mom had delivered you here—placenta and blood—mark registered on our sands, not cis-sarju, if you get me. Gotra-ghetto-thinking must be quite incestuous. But I have drifted, Mama.

I now fear that I may be going the way Dad did. Living on two shores brings its problems. I love it more there, I was born abroad, but now I am worried that the alluvial tug of the

Gangetic plain is getting to me. Home and homeland are like a mother, you can't have homelands in pairs. But I will live with it. Father did not. God saw to it that he died in Lucknow and there were more than three hundred mourners at the Gomati bank and at least half the pyre consisted of sandalwood logs. It was a calm winter evening, cloudless sky. He had asked me in his last days what I wanted of his property. I said I have enough. Leave what you can to Shail.

And talking of family one day Nishant told me as he returned from office that his sister would be coming to Delhi the next day. 'You should have told me this earlier,' I said. 'I'll get the guest room ready.' 'No,' he said, 'they are not staying with us. They already have a flat on Asaf Ali Road, her father-in-law's.' Jijaji, that is, her husband Vikramsheel, was planning to open a clinic here in Daryaganj, right place to make money. They are shifting to Delhi. 'Lovely' I said, though I didn't feel too good. She had come to Lucknow once after we had got married and were staying in Dilkusha Colony in a government flat—Nishant's male ego would not permit him to stay in my kothi, for he would have looked a *ghar jamai*. She was at least five years older than Nishant which would mean a decade older than me. I thought I had taken good care of her, taking her around to the Imambaras and the Rumi Gate and showing her the Residency (she wasn't a bit interested in history). Nishant drove her to Kakori, for what good reason I don't know, except that she thought she would recall the Kakori conspiracy, when all we saw was a slightly seedy casbah.It was winter and the only visit she enjoyed was to the Coleus-and-Chrysanthemum show at the Botanical Gardens. She hardly smiled, and a serious face sat rather ill on her stocky body.When she left she hadn't bothered to say a word of thanks to me.

The Wheels Grind Slow

Politically, things were getting messier. The fifty-odd commissions set up by the Janata government had nothing much to show. Mrs G was, of course, sent to jail amidst high drama. She played cat and mouse with the team of flatfoots sent to arrest her, now moving into another room to collect some knick knack and now going to the washroom and bolting the door. Who can object if you bolt the washroom door? The sons, Rajiv and Sanjay, in their Pajeros chased the arresting team right up to Tihar jail. Nishant was visibly shaken and I relented, in the sense I put a stop to my relentless diatribes. The Janata government thought the people would be satisfied once she was jailed, as promised by them. The only promises politicians keep in India Mama, are jailing their opponents once they come to power. As for the jobs they promised and the sops to the labour movement and stern action against criminals, you may as well forget it. They didn't calculate how sentimental the Indians are. The eyes of the women turned watery, not because they were stung by the smoke in the kitchen, but on seeing Mrs Gandhi sent to jail. This was not what they wanted to see. They were no part of an audience around an amphitheatre, their souls cleansed by watching *Antigone*. The black-and-white TVs touched a vein of national compassion no one thought existed. And they started doubting the statements, twenty-seven to the dozen, of the Georges and Raj Narayans and Madhu Limyes day after day. They treated what these leaders said with the disdain reserved for slogans coined a week before elections. Under the skin of words there was no blood, sub-cutaneous anaemia Mama.

There was no hidden code to this change of mood. The clamour from the party leaders did the trick—and the bickering. The people disapproved, and harboured their dislike against this vendetta, as they perceived it, against a forlorn woman. The national euphoria which had brought the party in had just collapsed.

The Greeks had a wheel of fortune they believed in. Wheels have to turn Mama, or why have wheels. And pardon my asides, if our planet was square, it wouldn't have been wheeling around the sun—must ask an astronomer. Wish I could have dated Copernicus! I sat in an auto the other day, returning from the South Extension market, and the driver asked me, 'Mem Sahib, *yeh salay kar kya rahen hain*?' (What are these so and sos up to?) He was talking of the government, of course. When pejoratives get linked to the government you know something is wrong. And then he added, 'They won't last long'.

The fellow was a prophet. Next day the government started disintegrating, chaps jumped ship, they moved towards Charan Singh. The ostensible cause for the desertions was that they could not work with Jana Sangha members, who also belonged to the RSS, an organization suspected perhaps erroneously (who knows?)of sporting a hidden Hitlerite moustache, though how a moustache can be hidden is anyone's guess. No one has accused them of a Mussolini paunch as yet. A falling government is like a huge landslide Mama, first some debris rolls down the hillside, then there's a tremor which only the sensitive can feel, (mules and mountain ponies can smell it from afar, instinctively) and then the crash, mud-slime gathering pace as it rolls down in cahoots with gravity. During our conversations over the Janata fiasco my husband did not gloat. The civil service gets used to routine; it doesn't like jerk and *jhatka*, if you know what I mean. Stability, status quo, same idiot or scoundrel in dhoti kurta to look up to, his personal eccentricities known, his love for *methi-ka-paratha* for instance—that's the ideal air-conditioned, politically-conditioned atmosphere he is comfortable with. He never commiserated, thank God. Then, out of nowhere, it occurred to him to mention that Zulfiqar Ali Bhutto had been arrested in Pakistan. Murder charge no less. 'You are showing me two maps Nishant, comparing us with Pakistan and implying we still are better off even as we blunder along. Is that it? A government with a massive mandate falls within two years. How does that change anything? Our politicians have let us down. Let the Pakistanis handle their murder and crime and probable regicide as best as they can.'

Six months, an election and a chastened Indira Gandhi was back in power. Of course, I realized that things would change for the better as far as we were concerned. Husbandji did not want to show me his little glimmer of glee. But he was driving all over the place, making political contacts. Efforts never go waste. He was picked up by a minister from Bihar. Bihari water is quite special but Bihari blood is thicker than even water. He was now joint secretary in the ministry and secretary to the minister. Initially all he would say into the phone was 'Sir,

Sir'. Slowly that changed. He was soon speaking in Hindustani to his boss, now and then even cracking a joke. Within six months he was handling the minister's personal affairs, and one Saturday he even brought the great man's cheque book home. 'How come?' I asked. 'Well, I am writing his cheques, a good dozen, he just has to sign. He is paying back an overdraft from the bank, sending a cheque for his property tax and so on. Don't bother your head with all this.'

He was going with the minister abroad now and the bar was getting well stocked—two Johnnie Walker Black Labels a trip. Soon that stopped. He was getting exotic whiskies now. I noticed a Talisker, single malt from the Isle of Skye. These were the early eighties Mama, I didn't know what single malt meant, by which I mean I had no idea what was so great about a single malt. Once in a week or so I would sip a glass of wine, but that was it. I benefitted now and then—a perfume here, once even a chiffon lace sari. His minister took no one but him on his foreign jaunts. He headed two ministries. Once he returned from a tour of West Germany and next day as I was putting away his coat I found a Swiss Air boarding card for Zurich, Frankfurt to Zurich. In the evening I let it drop casually that I thought he was going to West Germany. That's right he answered and I thought I had put him off a bit. After a gulp or two of his whiskey he said, 'Why did you ask?' I had no option but to be frank now. 'You never said anything about going to Zurich,' I said. He was startled, I could tell though he didn't want to show it. He didn't ask how I came to know, but kept looking into his glass like a sibyl staring at a bowl of coffee grounds. 'I was brushing your coat this morning and found your boarding card.'

'The minister had to go there, a private affair of his. Never talk about it.' And he shook his head in dismay. I refrained from joking about the 'affair.' Even a street urchin would tell you why a minister had to go to Zurich or Geneva. After this incident I made it a point not to touch his coat once he returned from a trip. A coat being brushed or a boarding card sticking out of a pocket are no big deal Mama, it's just like a fly falling in a jug of milk. Our parties became more chic and friends looked out for them. Then disaster struck. Sanjay Gandhi died as his plane crashed during stunts in the air. The paparazzi zeroed in on how Mrs Gandhi had gone looking for keys at the accident site. Disasters come in pairs, sometimes in threes. A few days later days later, Nishant's minister went down a mine to see for himself the conditions under which miners worked, and never came back. I mean did not come out alive. They wasted time trying to revive him. When they took him to the hospital he was declared 'brought dead'.

Gloom all around. This was not some sundry political boss kicking the bucket. He was from Bihar, from the same *biradari*, caste, as Nishant, and Hubby was damn good at work, everyone said so, no wonder he was the favourite of the politico. A month after the minister died, Nishant was transferred to the Agricultural Ministry. Within a month he was off on a tour—again abroad this time. 'So you are in with the minister of your new ministry as well?' I asked. He just shrugged his shoulders. He was hardly away for three or four days and was back.

Balbir Uncle Takes Ill

It was a telegram. Balbir Uncle had fallen ill and he was in Kangra, his cottage next to his vast apple orchard. He was down with pneumonia and a severe one at that. My only uncle! I bolted to Kangra. It was good to be back, even the birds had a clearer note. His estate, if I could call it such, was much better than our little cottage with the scabbed lawn which my father had left me. This estate of his was his baby, he had nursed it for over twenty years. Next to the cottage were mandarin trees, I loved looking at those little golden orbs lighting up every branch. He loved making a jam out of them, a hybrid preservative, half marmalade and half jam. He had, against advice, also put up a bed of lavender flowers. He had grown the purple haze lavender, but the deep blue of the flowers had faded a bit under the Indian sun. They had a mauve touch about them now.

I thought to myself that the shadows of the purple flower and the withered leaf were alike black. Remembered a poetic fragment from the past—

'Naked to earth was I brought.
Naked to earth I'll descend.
Why should I labour for naught
seeing how naked the end?'

Memory, in tune with my bleak mood, had ejected these lines from where, I wouldn't know. I noticed his apricot trees, the branches weighed down by the fruit. When I was a kid we used to break the kernel on the grindstone and eat the almond within, often bitter. It had rained earlier and I walked up to the glazed veranda, the black humus giving way beneath my flat shoes.

He was well looked after, had a night nurse and a male day nurse. Within three days he was better, the phlegm had lessened, and he was breathing freely. We could talk at last which was a relief. 'We seldom talk about the family,' he said. 'We should. Your mother for instance, how much do you know about her?' I kept quiet. He thought you were exceptionally intelligent Mama, not just the way you picked up languages like skewering fish fingers with a tooth pick and swallowing them, his words. He was impressed by the manner in which you majored in philosophy. He added you put in very hard work as well but the really remarkable thing was the way you got to the core of Marx or any other philosopher you tackled. 'Philosophers sometimes don't know themselves what they want to say, and even if they do, they find it tough to exit from the morass of knowledge they have gathered and the flood of things that come to their mind which they want to express. They get caught in the swamp of their own making and their outpourings are seldom pithy and never very clear. A philosophic tract is a cloud and often at the end of it there is no rain. But you could have come out with a series of books—*Marx Made Easy*, *Immanuel Kant Made Easy*.

'She was also clever. The way she played that Markham along was a lesson, reminded me of a woman carrying on with two lovers, communism on the one hand and the foreign office or the secret service on the other. And she did it in such a languid manner, spinning the Americans round her fingers. Her loyalty towards the communist cause was fierce, steady, unrelenting. Or was it?'

He seemed to relapse into silent contemplation, almost appeared to be in need of it, a respite from his own definitive opinions. 'I mentioned that she could get to the heart of things…'

'Core,' I interjected. 'Yes core,' he continued. 'She got there dealing with others. I am not sure if she ever got to the core of her own feelings.'

'What are you trying to say, Uncle?'

'I am hesitating, Seema. Who am I to talk about the core of another person's feelings, especially if I am saying that she herself couldn't get a grip of the deepest currents of her inner turmoil, something that swirls inside you and you can't give it a name? I am also conscious that I am talking to her daughter.' I persisted however, you can't say that much and then clam up, can you. Now I have a right to know. Spill it out, Uncle.

'I think Seema, it is just a guess, for a good part of a decade she was nursing romantic notions towards MN.' Then he clammed up, leaned back on the sofa, and I heard him wheezing, like air slowly hissing out of a punctured tyre. I couldn't control myself, seldom can. 'What the hell do you mean by "nursing romantic notions" Uncle (I was insolent enough to mimic him!)? Are you saying that she was in love with him? Then why the hell don't you say so!' He laughed and so did I, his only niece saying all this. We sat there in silence for a while watching a pair of jet black birds pecking away at insects in the lawn. After about fifteen minutes of watching birds and a horse chestnut falling on the lawn and a troupe of monkeys invade the grounds only to be shooed off by the gardener, I finally asked, 'What makes you say that Uncle?'

'Russian. After she majored in political philosophy, she went for Russian. Why on earth? She wasn't making a career as an expert on Bolshevism. She wasn't a journalist writing for papers. What was Bukharin to her or she to Bukharin, or Trotsky for that matter, that she should wade into this Slavic language? It was MN. She wanted to be useful to him, near him. Isn't that another word for love?'

'What about loyalty? Uncle, can't you think of passionate loyalty, devotion which big leaders command through their charisma. Can't that be an explanation?'

'Seema, how old were you when your father died?'

'Fifteen years.'

'He was ten years older than your mother. He was as tall as MN and as dignified. He was a substitute for her first love...I am sorry don't cry.' Of course I was crying, any daughter would cry to hear this and see the unremitting logic behind it.

'Seema I am sorry, but have you read the journal which I gave you when you came to write your book which you never wrote, some Pahari painting wasn't it?' I told him I didn't have the courage. How would I know what she had written? 'Your mother has written about her childhood and more. Go back and read it.'

I wished at that moment I had a sister, or, second choice, even a brother. You can discuss your parents with your sister or brother, who else? There's none other. He was wheezing a bit and I helped him to get back to his bed. As a parting shot he said, 'You haven't read the journal I gave you. A bit of what I said is evident from the journal.'

I sat down in the lawn. Memory turned up an old scene,

I must have been seven or so, a photograph placed before me and a forefinger (father's?) pointing out ancestors, saw the family framed, and I: why is the photograph brown? Father: child this is sepia, afflicts old photographs; I don't know the word sepia, but keep quiet, old stratagem of mine, never exhibit your ignorance; I just ask why, why what he asks, why does it turn brown, and find he is at a loss for words; the window behind the old family is open, the landscape against which they are framed looks haggard; was distance brown in those days I ask; laughter; father's explanation goes over my head, it is a signature of the times, they are captive in a six by four frame, they are captives to an age gone by. Were cameras similar to ours, I ask and I remember his answer, the shutter dropped as it does now, and the lens had a good eye, till filmed by a cataract. Why can't the old speak in phrases children can understand?

I went back to my cottage in the evening, the one Dad had left me, couldn't stand Balbir Uncle for a while. I made my excuses—had to see things were ok and clean and if the caretaker was looking after the place. But the weather had changed; a cloud as solid as old age bronze was making straight for us. Thunder was still distant, a growl from the other side of infinity. Uncle tried to dissuade me but I insisted. We wasted a half hour bickering. Rain started pelting away as I stepped into Balbir's car and I saw the driver shrugging shoulders—what can you do if the woman is mad? I noticed the hiss of tyres in the night rain. Rain slanted in, the cold seemed to have hardened the drops. I noticed the mist around the street lamps, till the interior of the car became thick with moisture and even the wipers were of no help. I lowered the side window, never mind getting wet, and that seemed to be of some help. When the driver objected, I told him visibility was more important than getting wet. We were moving so slowly that I noticed two wet dogs following a wet bitch, as they got lit up by the headlights. I tipped the driver as I got off. He hollered for the caretaker-cum-maali and all was well, even though the rain was roaring against the tiles. Late at night, the rain relented and instead of the roar, I thought I heard the sibilance of water drizzling from the skies.

Mother's Journal (1910–1920)

'I can't take the land with me but I can sell it.' That was father at his sharpest. I had never heard him speak to mother in any but the kindest of tones, sometimes as if a loving elder was talking to a child. The rebuff was in answer to mother saying this is all you've got, this piece of black soil. (She didn't know the word 'alluvial', or she would have used it here.) You can't take it to Canada. This had come at the end of a long drawn argument to which I, about ten years old fiddling nervously with my plaits, was a mute witness. Mother had started it saying nobody abandons land. Land is life, home, blood, country! Blood is spilled on borders, tell me why? Because it is the country's land. You are abandoning your own! She couldn't believe it.

Even when father's decision fell like a slap on her face, mother wasn't going to give in without a fight. 'Take it from me, you can't abandon a language also. You mean to say she (and she pointed furiously towards me) will speak in *git-pit*? Suppose she forgets Hindustani?' 'She won't,' father interrupted her patiently, but mother was furious. 'How will I speak with her, tell me, how will I? Step-mothers, *sauteli* moms, find it difficult to speak to their daughters. When these *vilayat*-returned shameless men bring a mem as a second wife, they can't speak to the husband's daughter. But I will not be able to speak to my own!'

Father didn't lose patience, didn't slap his head or roll his eyes (no one did in those days) just stood there silently allowing the storm to blow over. Which it did. Years later when I recalled the scene, it struck me that could mother have been nursing the fear that one dark day he would bring a Canadian dame home.

Mother was worried about *kala pani*, caste, excommunication. She never mentioned all this but we could sense it, father and I. Once when she casually let it drop father just said, 'We are not Brahmins.' You never could keep mother quiet.

'We are Thakurs, and are blessed that we can feed the *bhooka* Brahmin.'

'They are not as hungry as you think they are.'

Father couldn't be bothered about all this—touch and taboo. He had heard how Canadians gobble beef and ham, and was not averse to try both once he left our shores. There was no caste to lose in Canada, he thought, and if you did lose the damned thing, you couldn't make enquiries in Lost and Found. (All this he told me with his usual sarcasm decades later, during his year-long sickness, a precursor to his death.)

A good thing was we weren't Muslims—we didn't have any ancestors buried here, with a forlorn flame teetering over a stone slab, till the night wind snuffs it out. How can Muslims leave their lands and the bones of their dead? The wrench must be much greater. They think of exile as Hijr, smearing the dislocation with a shade of the sacral, Muhammad moving to Medina. I remember the rice—no one called it paddy those days, and a lily pond built lovingly by father. In a way he had sculpted the land, the boundary fringed with bramble and camel thorn. There were more than forty acres of rice, and he also grew corn and gram near a grove of shisham trees. He had his scarecrows there. Even I would help in setting up a scarecrow, putting a small earthen pot over his head and painting it—the moustache bigger than the face.

We had more than rice, of course. In our holding we had an old broken wall holding up the ruins of a Naubat Khana where sometime or other shehnais must have wailed in welcome to a wedding or a birth, the players, their cheeks ballooning, swaying to the whine of the ungainly looking instrument. Much of the plaster had peeled off and the thin old brick of previous years was visible. Two rickety pillars stood giving it tentative support, and a wall in the rear. It was anyone's guess if the Naubat Khana was holding up the wall or the other way around. The two of them could be likened to a pair of drunks holding on to each other so that they didn't fall.

No one taught us about hierarchies, we just picked all that up—I mean I did. It was as smooth and natural as the eye telling you that the earth is brown and leaves are green and sunsets are lined with gold. The Baheliyas, the hunters, were never to be allowed indoors and the kills which they brought—a leg of a buck, or a nilgai, or sand grouse were to be left outside. Meat incidentally was never cooked in the kitchen. It was cooked out in the open on a wood fire in a special vessel which was never allowed into the kitchen and was cleaned and scrubbed with wood ash outside the house. Mother and I never touched any meat. Only father did, and with considerable relish. It was lower caste women who touched meat. Mother said they would be born even lower on the caste scale next time they were unfortunate enough to be born, and if the world was unfortunate enough to receive them once again.

The Kachis who grew vegetables could come to the house and squat on the veranda with their turnip and cabbage and aubergine—the Kachis were as dark as the brinjal. They were given an annual sack of rice. So were the two Baheliyas. Rice straw was free—people carried it away as they liked, a straw pile became their bed. Father wasn't bothered about touch, especially when he went for shikar with Baheliyas and bird catchers. And he kept telling mother not to drill her ideas into my head. To be fair to mother, she laughed and chatted with the women who came to thresh rice and later pound it in those thick cylindrical iron vessels. Once when he was looking the other way I asked father, 'Who are these rice pounders?' What caste they were, was left unsaid. The way he moved his head and fixed me with a cold stare reminded me of a bison turning its head to eye a hunter. 'Women,' he barked. A minute later he pointed at the Kachis watering the fields and added, 'And these are men, just like us. Understand?'

There were omens—there always are for those who want to believe in them. There was a falcon's nest in one of our trees and the male would sit on a fork and never bother about us. One evening the baaz, as we called him, flew away at our approach, shooting up vertically into the sky. Next morning we set out for Mathura to celebrate Janm Ashtami, the birth of Krishna. I didn't like the look of a string of women in white, their heads shaved, most of them begging. When mother refused to answer my questions, I told her I knew. They were widows. Mother clamped her hand over my mouth. Mother felt thirsty and drank the water and it tasted brackish. She spat it out. I gulped it down. On return I fell ill, the whites of my eyes turning yellow. A Muslim Fakir was called and he prayed over me, put his palms over my eyes and left a bowl of water under the bed. Next morning the water had turned yellow and my fever abated. Mother said first the water turns salty, then yellow. Now all we need is for the water to turn black—kala pani, crossing the ocean, is what she meant.

Mother's real complaint was that father was too educated. You don't need college if you want to farm. You can't grow rice or wheat if your mind is busy cramming up. Education meant English and notes about this mountain range and that valley—a sierra here and the Andes there, and all of it learnt by rote. What had the Andes to do with transplanting rice? She didn't mind his maths and his hard-nosed bargaining at the grain mart—mandi—as he sold the crop. A train of bullock carts would carry the rice, while the straw would be carried away by the villagers. This was UP, The United Provinces of Agra and Oudh in 1910. We, of course, called it Avadh, our Avadh, the British called it Oudh.

There were other hurdles to be crossed before you could sell the land. But father mollified her. The land has to go to the daughter—that means to the in-law's family. It will never be in the Brajbir Singh name. Mother didn't have an answer to that. She hadn't had a son in ten years of marriage.

Father had left for Canada a year earlier, may have been more than a year. He had gone to explore. His English was okay, so there was no problem. It is full of Punjabis, he said when he returned. They were helpful, but they were not his people, men from the doab. It was only when he fell ill during his old age that he confided in me what he was up to. He found just Sikhs there. They were good to him; he didn't have to spend on food for the first month. The Sikhs didn't expect the cold insolence with which they were initially treated in Canada. People looked askance at these long haired immigrants who didn't know a word of English. Why did they expect any better, asked the old man, just because they had been declared a martial race by the British? The British treated everyone like that, including their own lower classes—the char woman and the chimney sweeper. They would use the term 'martial races' when it came to war. He was certain war was coming. How can anyone live with the snobbish English? Surely the Germans wouldn't. He also laughed at Teja Singh in Vancouver who was very worried about the *mowna lehar*, the wave of hair cutting and shaving among Sikh immigrants. Why couldn't they just trim their beards and be done? They looked handsome in their turbans. But the Khalsa Diwan was scared about the hat epidemic—the Bhai Bhag Singh and Bulwant Singh Granthi types. Six hundred Sikhs in Vancouver had started wearing hats! Disaster—*barbadi*—was round the corner! Father told me he empathized with both, the topiwalahs and the *granthies*.

Once we got there—wife and daughter, bed roll and steel trunk—mother never uttered a word of complaint, no matter how miserable she was. You can't keep a husband on the defensive all the time. Father had forbidden her from carrying any idols, including the one of Durga that she loved. But she had secretly smuggled that in, as also a six inch Ganesh, elephant head, large ears and all, in silver if you please. And she picked up words, the way you pick up an allergy these days. There was no such thing as an allergy in 1910. On being questioned by a kindly gori lady, I heard her answer looking the questioner square in the eye: 'Me doesn't English.' I was sent to a school, English was nothing new to me for I had studied in a decent school in Lucknow, but the accents were new, this English sounded like a completely alien tongue to me initially. Slowly, without being conscious of it, I started mimicking them, my 't's and 'd's got sharper, and once I was immersed in this river of clipped consonants, it was bliss, I shed some of my self-consciousness. Accents and self-consciousness have a lot to do with each other, more so if you are brown and your schoolmates white.

There was no recrimination from mother even in our first winter when her skin cracked and the land was blanketed with snow. At night, if the wind was right, it carried the howl of the pack to your ears. The first time we heard it, she quickly put the *razai* over my face to snuff out the sound, and I had to fight her off. 'Am old enough to hear wolves,' I snapped at her in English, my eyes blazing. Her smile was beatific, an acknowledgement of my having grown up. Mother's belly had started bulging unaccountably. I noticed she was eating less. Then I caught on. Father would look anxiously as she walked, ready to spring to her assistance, in case she wobbled. He would hold her hand as she walked down from the house to the road. I remember the day my brother was born. The sky had started rumbling with discontent since early morning, hours before dawn. A storm was in the offing as we set out for the hospital. She wanted a midwife but father insisted she had to move to a hospital and hired a horse carriage. We plied her with shawls and blankets. Snow and wind blew into the horse's face. At times an exceptionally fierce gust would shake the carriage. The nurses at the hospital were kind and warm. One of the sisters said, 'What a day to be born! Am certain a blizzard will be upon us shortly.' They made her change and put on hospital clothes and said none of these shawls and blankets would be permitted inside. They thought they carried germs and they threw them in a tub of boiling water, soap suds bouncing all over and circling the brim. Father kept absolutely quiet. The place was a revelation, the floor so clean with a glassy shine on it that reflected my face as I looked down. I had never seen anything like it. Men folk who knew us cursorily, all Sikhs, came to the hospital to be with us. They seemed more bothered about the outcome, whether it would be a boy or girl. Father's face remained impassive, he seemed more worried about mother.

It was a boy—he made us wait till midnight. Father said he is blizzard-born. I will name him with two B's, and he lit upon the name Balbir, but mother would have none of it. 'It is not a Hindu name,' she said. But Balbir it was and he remained Balbir for the rest of his life.

The boys in school looked at me as if I was a strange animal. No one made an attempt to talk. I thanked God for that. Three months later the headmaster called me, a grizzled hulk, a bit unkempt, tie hanging loose around his unbuttoned collar, pince-nez fitted precariously around his eyes, veiling the kindness dripping from those two windows.

'Do you find any of this of interest, kid?' He was pointing to my books.

'Any of what?'

'The subjects we teach.'

'Yes, but I want to learn is languages.'

'Languages!' His eyebrows shot up half an inch.

'Spanish.'

'Spanish? Where did you hear the word, not in India I am sure.'

I nodded my head.

'Better learn English first.'

'Learnt it, can talk to you.'(I must have sounded arrogant, chit of a girl with her plaits bound in a bun talking like that!)

'There's more to English than talking to an old wolf like me.'

'Kind wolf.' He laughed for a minute and said, 'Thank you. What's your name?'

'Shail.'

'Do you like it here?'

'Not sure.'

'Not sure if you like it?'No answer from me. 'What did your people do at home, in India?'

'Rice.'

'Rice!'

We grew rice, I said shamefacedly, carrying my palm to my lips.

'Nothing to be ashamed of. Be it rice, millet or wheat, anyone growing food is doing good to the planet.'

I liked the sound of Spanish, softer, a sibilance slipping into another almost surreptitiously like a lover's arm around your waist. A Mexican taught Spanish to a handful of us. I loved it, also because I wasn't the laggard anymore. We were all beginners. I looked forward to this one period a day.

Father, with the money from the land he had sold, had opened a grocery and was doing well. But he hated it. To be a shop owner was the last thing Thakur Brajbir Singh ever wanted. Mother had picked up enough English to work in the shop, though her consonants were thick, the 't's and 'd's sounding like an axe under a grinder. Life wasn't easy by any means. The Canadians, large sized all—even their strays were big—looked down upon us. There was nothing much to look up to us either, to be frank. Father would slap his forehead when he saw some of the immigrants walking on the street, unkempt and in dhotis. The Punjabi *jutti*, the slipper with an upturn, like the moustache of a zamindar villain in an Indian movie these days, was also a constant. Turban and beard did not endear them to the whites. And the *kirpan* belts were a veritable red rag. The Canadians didn't mind a hood packing a pistol in a holster, that could be called civilized (Al Capone would shortly be on the scene in Chicago) but a dagger dangling near the hip! Ex-service men alone wore shirt and pant, but they got lost in the jutti-and-dhoti crowd. Father would rather be dead than stir out in pyjamas, and I remember he kept his belt buckle shining. Mother never veered from her sari or salwar kameez.

Once I recall we saw a coffin being taken in a horse carriage, a black coffin, coachman and two others also dressed in black. Mother sensed what it was but still asked, what is it that they are taking in that long box. Father explained it was a coffin. She was appalled. 'Don't they carry their dead on their shoulders?' Father explained to her the graveyard was more than a mile off, and it was winter and the coffin was made of pine wood and heavy.

Father had made a few friends among the Sikhs—there were hardly any Hindus there—the crowd consisted of people from Punjab fleeing plague and famine. I would eavesdrop on the muttered conversation between Father and Harnam Singh Makkar and one Gobind Bihari. Gobind worked at Port Moody but would come in on weekends. I hadn't heard of plague earlier. However, many decades later, I came across the death figures in a journal. The lieutenant governor of Punjab reported to the governor general that plague was taking away 60,000 a week during some years preceding our coming to

Vancouver. They did not refer to it as Ton, as we did in Avadh. For the Punjabis it was mahamari, the great pestilence, the great killer. Harnam Singh said the stricken would be left out of the house like cattle and within hours they would be dead and the Kanjars would take the bodies away. How the Kanjars managed to escape disease and death remained a matter of wonder for him. When Bihari and Harnam Singh got emotional (which was always) they blamed the Englishmen even for the plague. All that digging to put through canals in Punjab, made all the ratty diseases come out in the open, they said. The Angrez can never leave well alone. There was always anti-Angrez talk.

After a year, father opened a saw mill and would smell of larch and pine even after a bath. We moved into another dingy apartment, the entire building looking like a rundown warehouse, but it had a chimney, though it was black as hell. It was a part of an indeterminate neighbourhood which was neither Canadian nor wholly ours. We started burning pine logs now instead of the cones which we used to gather for our first winter. I would gaze, enraptured, at some of the Canadian houses of the rich, the front vine-covered, garden immaculate, manicured. Wouldn't it be heaven to live in one of these?

Even in the new apartment we could hear the muttered goings on between father and Harnam Singh and at least one or two others. Once the news came in about the assassination attempt on the Viceroy, the excitement was electric. A lot of people came to our door. I was amused to see them looking over their shoulder as if they were a part of the bomb conspiracy. News came in dribs and drabs. The Viceroy was attacked as he returned from the great Durbar in December 1912, where King George V and his queen Mary took the salutes of the native princes. The English royalty was seated high on a balcony while the native royalty, one by one was called upon to give their 'farshi salaams', the spine slightly bent and the right arm moving from floor to chin. The princes in their brocades and turbans which sported scintillating solitaires, then had to back pedal half a dozen steps—it wouldn't do to show their arses to the Angrez royalty. There was much laughter in the house on that one. 'Was this George Panjum homosexual?' chortled Harnam Singh. I laughed and mother slapped me on the shoulder and asked me to go to another room where I wouldn't be able to hear what was going on.

There was much talk of rising up against both the Indian princes and the Angrez. The bomb attack on the viceroy, Lord Charles Hardinge, in Chandni Chowk was welcomed and the men drank a bottle of whisky for once instead of the fiery rum. '*Uthao jam, Qatil ke naam*,' they shouted as they raised their glasses. Lift up your glass for the assassin. The bomb was hurled at the haudah, killing the mahaut—the elephant driver—but only injuring the viceroy. Lady Hardinge escaped unhurt. Harnam Singh was happy about that—nothing should happen to the *zenani*. The best part was that the bomb-throwers vanished without a trace. But he bemoaned the fact that we didn't have good bombs. The Viceroy should have been thrown off the elephant with the blast, he said. It was rumoured that one of the assailants was a woman, and for days I would be day dreaming of chucking a bomb (had never seen one though) at a beetroot red British official. Rebellion was in the air. We lived with it as one lives with the aroma of home-made bread.

Once mother made bold to ask as to why we were getting entangled in this Punjabi war? Father said forcefully, 'India's war'. And he stared at her for a good minute. He could be short with others too. Once Harnam Singh talked of Majbi Sikhs derisively and father shut him up.

Nothing lasts. War clouds were closing in. Before war, rumours, before the rumours, omens, columns in newspapers, martial music and patriotic songs—that is the sequence. Forgot one thing—lots of *gaali*s, swear words against the enemy, what monsters they are. I would hear the word 'Ghadar' in the confabulations between father and Harnam Singh and Gobind Bihari. The community in Vancouver kept getting more hostile to the British as the Canadians started baying, if not for our blood, certainly for our exit; and certainly for the doors to be shut to any bearded rustics wearing sarongs instead of pants. As it is they were fed up with the Chinese and the Japanese immigrants and this sudden influx of Sikhs with a sprinkling of other Indian communities, was the last straw for Canadian white labour. The Asians were depressing the wages. Throw them out they said. And then came Komagata Maru, Japanese ship commandeered by the Sikhs, with a paymaster called Gurdit Singh Sandhu. The radio was silent about the long voyage, but the grapevine substituted admirably: three hundred and seventy-six people aboard, ship sailing from Hong Kong, Shanghai, some Japanese port on to Vancouver. It was 23rd May, 1915. It was illegal they said. What is illegal about it? Asked the small Indian community. It has picked up passengers en route, which it was not supposed to, said the authorities, and it has been met by Ghadarites—Bhagwan Singh Gyani and Barkatullah. Indians answered that Bhagwan Singh is our high priest in Vancouver, though we knew that he was involved with the Ghadar—the new US-Canadian party wanting freedom for India. The language was more sonorous those days, the Ghadarites wanted to 'cast off the shackles of imperialism'. (And no one spoke of the sea as sea, it was always 'the azure mane'.) Ghadar incidentally was also the name given by the British to the 1857 uprising.

The ship was to dock at the Burrod inlet, what was actually the Coal Harbour, barely two hundred meters off the CPR Pier A. We were trying to get there to give them a tumultuous welcome. Our hearts sank when the news came that the Immigration officers led by Fred 'Cyclone' Taylor had gone on ship to meet the Japanese Captain. 'Cyclone' was bad news, tough fellow—tough types mould themselves in their image, rather the image of themselves they want to see in the mirror. Cyclone told the Japanese captain to vamoose. The Canadians thought of the ship passengers as a sort of epidemic that was to disembark and invade their land. The Mounted Police was brandishing their truncheons to keep us and the welcoming Sikhs away from the dock. A doctor and his family were allowed to disembark because they had gone back to India for a holiday. The doctor told us the others would be sent back. All the way back, some of us cried in horror? He nodded. Father tried to get across the gangplank but was threatened by an uplifted arm with a truncheon at the end of it. The horses were getting fidgety—they had probably never encountered something like this, for now we started shouting slogans of '*Inqalab zindabad! Nadir Shahi nahin chalegi! Tana Shahi nahi chalegi!*' (I still have to find out who Tana Shah was.) Regrettably horse and mount did not understand our lingo; they had never been close to sloganeering Hindustani. The ship would be turned back into the maw of the ocean, some of us were convinced. Horse and truncheon meanwhile managed to turn us back from the Coal Harbour.

As we went home that evening, father said we will also be pushed out. He didn't eat his evening meal. Mother unaccountably vented her spleen on father for taking me along to the welcoming party. Father would sometimes remain quiet at mother's unreasonable recriminations. I had to tell her, who knew they would almost beat us back? The goras will never allow it, said mother, feeding off a vein of pessimism innate in all mothers. The ship lay at anchor for two months. There was a time when the Canadians would not allow any water or food to reach the ship. A Shore Committee was formed by Hassan Rahim and Sohan Lal Pathak. Father, Harnam Singh and Gobind Bihari all pitched in with money which the committee asked off the community and over 20,000 dollars were collected. Canadian MPs came and they too addressed public meetings shouting that no Indian would be allowed. There were confabulations in the house. The ire of the people was directed against Hopkinson of the Police or immigration—the community hardly knew the administrative set up here. Most Indians had hardly been in Canada for more than six or eight years, most had come in 1906. There were mutterings that he had some Punjabi sources and was feeding the government of Columbia with the information that the boat people had many rebels who would create chaos in Canada. The High Court endorsed the government and one day the Harbour tugboat was asked to push the ship out to sea, but not before the frustrated passengers had vented their ire against the police by showering them with bricks and coal. The *Vancouver Sun* reported against 'Howling Hindus' who hurled their coal missiles in such a torrent that it looked as if the police had been under 'a coal chute'.

We will shortly be shoved out of here, said father, one

day and we started packing for America. We got a visit from the police. They wanted us out. Harnam Singh said he would never leave, even though he had a brother in California who was doing well. Yet, how people change. He came over shame-faced one evening. 'I have changed my mind,' he said. 'What about?' asked father. He was longing for his family in the village and so was his wife, missed the morning *Japji* in the gurdwara, longed for the rope mesh of the *manji* of all things. He justified his decision to go back with a Punjabi saw—Punjabi is good both with expletives and saws.

> *Jai sukh Chajju de chubare*
> *Na Balkh na Bukhare*
>
> The bliss at Chajju's rundown shack (chubara)/
> cannot be matched by Balkh or Bukhara.

❁

Can shadows be displaced? We were. Shifts are not easy, especially moving across countries. Each shift has an underlying narrative that may or may not open itself to language. Does one call it a plurality of exiles or crossing borders or a ride through a continent? Memory is an outcrop of ancient weed and I have to cut through it. Our four years, or was it five, were over. I had picked up my English and didn't have to affect an accent anymore. I was almost speaking like the Canadians. Mother was happy at that but often put on a sour face as she asked father how on earth she was going to understand her child! I had picked up Spanish and the Mexican teacher placed me on top of the class. Balbir was four when we left Vancouver and couldn't understand why I was crying. Mother scolded me as always. 'This is not our land. You should have cried when we left Avadh, but you were laughing! Ungrateful girl. This is not our land. This belongs to the goras and their mems.'

All our Sikh friends had relatives in California. But it was no fun. The shadow of war was hovering over half the world, and father said God knows what the British intelligence men have told the flatfoot American police. They stalked us, even me, as I finished my graduation. The British Police had sent a CID man to corner the 'rebels' and 'terrorists' as they termed the Indian revolutionaries. Most of the so-called revolution was talk, talk and more talk. Father again made friends with the kind of people who had that uneasy over-the-shoulder look when they were out in the streets. If you opened the door as they rang the bell, they weren't happy standing in the open and answering your queries. If mother was at the door she would ask for names and why they had come. They fidgeted and wanted to be indoors, roof and roof-shadow over their heads, no longer in the line of sight of supposed stalkers. Mother didn't care for them—she knew we were thrown out of Canada because of these baagis (rebels). Father corrected her and called them inqalabis (revolutionaries). She even asked father once whether we were ever going to have a settled home—quite willing to go back to our forty acres of rice and the crumble that was the Naubat Khana, only all that was no longer ours.

Of father's visitors and companions, what can I say? They had, of course, different names and faces and yet they were no different from the Gobind Biharis and the Harnam Singh Makkars of Vancouver—emotions always on the boil. How they cursed when news came in about that lethal firing. Near Calcutta, as the Komagata Maru completed its journey round the world, nineteen passengers were shot down at a place called Budge Budge by the Indian police. (The blame fell on the Indian sepoys who fired. 'For what *yaar*, for the measly ten rupees that they get as their salary!' 'They get fifteen!' '*Chad paray*, forget it, the Indian soldier will fight the Germans for eleven rupees a month. Just you watch.' '*Thukdi gal hai*—it is all about prestige.' 'What prestige, killing your own people? All this is nonsense, *bakwas*. Look at Russia—socialism, anarchism, syndism…' 'Syndicalism, you mean.' '*O, kuch vi keh lo*, call it what you like, they are engineers of new systems. We only have *lohar*s, bloody blacksmiths. To throw a bad bomb at an elephant is all we can do.' 'I say first kill landlords—the ones who got lands for fighting for the British in 1857.' 'What nonsense, zamindars! First kill the Viceroy. Start from top.' 'Very difficult killing goras. Start with the desi boot-lickers first.') At its worst, that was the kind of stuff I heard across the walls, especially when people were in their cups. Father just listened. I was old enough to sometimes join the crowd now.

News filtering in from Vancouver raised our spirits up a bit. Whatever may have happened at Budge Budge, in Vancouver the Sikhs were not going to forget or forgive. Two of the informants were gunned down. Hopkinson must have known that he had it coming. Of course, a big cheer went up when news came that Hopkinson had been shot in the courthouse.

I thought it was amazing that the inqalabis could know about the CID Englishman who had come from India, and detect his footprints in the actions of the American police. Rumours about a revolutionary from India also floated around. His exploits were talked about in whispers, a bomb here, a pistol shot there, and even a shipload of guns trawling around the Indian Ocean littoral, all attributed to his name. Who could he be? No one mentioned his name, the way some tribes won't take the name of a sacred totem.

Father took me to New York and the Columbia University campus to hear Lala Lajpat Rai, all the while telling me what a great leader he was. How he railed against the British! How graphic was his description of Indian poverty. He used the word 'exploitation' about ten times in his talk. I was sorry that there were just about a hundred people to listen to him. After the meeting a gentleman I had seen with father once took us to meet the leader, who seemed fatigued after his one hour lecture. He was embittered. He had gone on ship to India but had been turned back from England, he told us. As the ship docked in England, policemen came aboard and accosted him. According to him the conversation went something like this:

British Police: 'I am Inspector Jeremy Hogan, Mr Rai. Would you make yourself available to answer a question or two?'

Lala Lajpat Rai: 'I don't think I have a choice.'

Inspector Hogan: 'May I know where you are heading to, Sir?'

Lala Lajpat Rai: 'You haven't asked any of the other passengers this.'

Police: 'We are specifically asking you Mr Rai, and if I may say so, for your own good.'

Lajpat Rai: 'Oh really? Since when has our good been of any interest to the British Police?'

Inspector Hogan: 'Am I to understand Sir, that this questioning is not to your liking?'

Lajpat Rai: 'It is not, Sir.'

Inspector Hogan: 'Oh, it isn't? To cut the Gordian knot, if you know what I mean by that Mr Rai, it would not be a good idea to head to India, if that's your objective. You may not be very welcome there.'

Lajpat Rai: 'Why not? My meetings are attended by thousands in India. Only some days before boarding this ship I got a news-cutting from an Indian newspaper, calling me "The Lion of Punjab"!'

Hogan: 'Caged lion, Sir.'

Lajpat Rai: 'Is that a warning from HMG?'

Hogan: 'HMG does not concern itself with people like you Mr Rai. It is the job of the British police to deal with trouble-makers conspiring against the Empire, an Empire which has done so much for poor Indians, if I may be bold enough to say so! Good day Mr Rai.'

'I took the hint and returned to America,' said the Leader.

In a matter of days war fell on us like a bomb—a Duke was killed somewhere (I had no idea then what an Archduke was) and the police started filling the jails with Indian 'revolutionaries' in America. Would our inqalabi visitors still talk of assassinating viceroys? I dared not ask the question, as father bundled us to the Mexican border in desperate haste to escape the American police.

Mexico! Thank God I knew Spanish. And, thank God, we didn't have to look over the shoulder. We settled into an apartment after father had changed his dollars to the Mexican Peso. I quote from my diary about the goings on during our first Sunday.

Father said 'I am tired. You go around, but find your way

back!' I wander through the streets, gawk at the churches. The service is on and I hear the choir, hesitate on the steps, mother had not let me enter a church in Vancouver. A young man watching me is rather amused and shouts in English, go in Lady, don't worry, its kosher, and follows me into the church. I don't know what kosher means. I am enthralled by the singing. When I come out he accosts me. 'Are you Catholic?' I shake my head. 'I am relieved,' he says, 'thought you may be hesitating because it may not be what it seems, a church to Virgin Mary. Have seen some of your nuns, pretty die hard. Aztec and Maya deities were worshipped along with Virgin Mary in this church once. Now of course we are unadulterated Christian, not that it is something to be extra proud of. Some like me would be quite happy with the earlier mix.' I am not taken aback, much to his disappointment.

He gives his name—Ramos; asks me if I would have coffee with him and we walk into an eatery. I find out he is a journalist; at the moment is concentrating on learning German. Why German, I ask, a bit intrigued. 'Must know both sides,' he says, 'and nothing like a language to tell you what a people are. Language is confession, of a culture, civilization without shirt and vest and, pardon me, underwear.'

He gets friendly, and mentions I must meet the Indian revolutionary, then clams up. I want more from him and feigning innocence, ask, 'Oh, the dangerous one?' He falls for the bait, shakes his head. 'What is so dangerous about revolutionaries? Only blood-suckers have to fear them, not you and I.' I nod, and repeat after him, 'You and I.' He goes on, 'First they rob the harvest, then the land, then they snatch the bead necklace from the peasant woman, she has nothing more classy than beads, though once their necks were loaded with gold. And then, as their ambitions rise, they think, why not the bloody nation itself? Why must I leave it for others to rob? The nation is just a bank without guards, don't you see?' I see, but still laugh. He shakes his head in disapproval. No laughing matter this. But he knew the revolutionary and he took me there, of course with father's permission. I had asked Ramos why he wanted me to meet the great man. He needs a secretary, he said. We met him. He was tall and stern-looking, I think the expression was put on.

Best to be frank right from the start. 'It's my father who is a communist. We, mother and I, are not into that sort of thing.'

'What sort do you mean? Revolutions, lady, change not just life but the world.'

I kept wondering at that moment which meant more to me, life or the world. Instead, all I said was, 'Revolutions fizzle out.' 'Yes,' he said, 'but they leave a mark. Look at 1812.' I didn't know what he was talking about.

He had a forbidding presence and he was curt, couldn't tell if it was put on, never know with great men. They're never far from thinking about the impression they create on crowds, followers et al, so why not aspiring secretaries? Ramos introduced me. He kept looking at his papers and momentarily deigned to fix me in fitful stares. It is a bit unnerving when a man is looking down and then, without raising his head, lifts up eyelid and brow to stare at you, expressionless. Ramos plonked himself on a chair and I followed.

'What has Ramos told you?'

'About what.'

'The kind of work you'll be involved in here.'

'Secretarial.'

'And what does that mean?'

I wasn't happy with the drift. 'I'd like to be frank, Sir. We both know what this sort of work is, paper, typing (I don't know shorthand), phone calls provided there's a phone (I looked around and saw one) and helping you in your work, whatever it is.'

He smiled for the first time. Ramos laughed. 'And what do you think my work is?'

'You tell me.' This time I laughed.

'You're pretty confident for a girl your age. And bold.'

'We are Thakurs. Father left a store and a sawmill in Vancouver after the Komagata Maru affair.'

He nodded. 'You fancy yourself a fighter for freedom, is it, inqalab zindabad type?'

'Not me. My father. Lots of talk in the house about shooting this Britisher and that Britisher.' And then I put my knife in. 'Wannabe revolutionaries are good with words.' Ramos gasped and the great man looked hard at me trying to gauge what exactly I was leading up to. I added, 'Father even took me to a meeting of Lala Lajpat Rai at the Columbia University ground, you know.'

'Meeting with Lojpot Roy?'

'No Sir, he was addressing an audience. We were a part of the audience, though later a Sikh gentleman took us in and we heard him again in private.'

'Very good people, the Sikhs. Do you speak Bengali?' I shook my head and told him we were from UP. 'How were you concerned with the ship?'

It was at that moment that a lady walked in from the kitchen, wiping her hands on her apron. 'With whom are you yacking away? Oh, hello Ramos,' and she smiled at him. Oh, so this was his wife.

'Evelyn, see whom Ramos has brought. Wants to work as our secretary.'

I bowed just a wee bit and she smiled at me warmly. 'Sorry my hands are wet, can't shake yours.'

MN repeated his question, 'What did you all have to do with the ship?'

'We went to the docks to welcome it. The police was ready to beat us up. The Canadians didn't want any Indians coming in.'

'People don't like poor immigrants. The rich would be welcome. Wealth has an entry pass most places.' It was his wife Evelyn who said that, nodding her head. I found myself getting bolder. 'The Canadian workers thought we would depress the wages further. As it is the Chinese workers had brought down the wages.'

'What were you up to in the States?'

'I graduated,' I said.

He looked at her and at Ramos, then after a pause he asked, 'When can you start?'

'Start what?' I shot back.

'Work, damn it.'

'Tomorrow. My father wants me home before dark.'

'All fathers do and Indian mothers wouldn't let you stir out of the house if they had their way. We'll see about that.'

I got up. As a parting shot I told him, 'And I am good at Spanish, so please don't worry on that score.'

'Hmm, you think well of yourself, don't you?'

'I do,' and we all laughed, as Ramos and I walked off. In the street I told Ramos, 'He never said a word about payment.'

'Don't worry. He is flush with money, I don't know how. But he has enough.'

'Better a well-to-do revolutionary than a starving one,' I said with a laugh, as we parted and he went his way.

That's how I began work with MN.

✲

He didn't seem to have the money. The plumbing was suddenly giving trouble, but he told me not to call the plumber, with Evelyn looking on disapprovingly. They never argued in my presence. I'll first need to go to the bank, he added. He did not ask me to connect him on phone, but phoned the German embassy himself, and I could notice the disappointment on his face when he couldn't speak to the person he was after. Evelyn walked out with a shopping bag for the groceries. He made another call, and must have got the man he was after for he bounded out of the office, directing me not to look out of the window. His apartment faced one of the broadest streets of *Colonia Roma* as the colony was named. It was an after-dusk moment and I switched off the lights and looked through the window so that no one could notice me. I gasped as I saw a car trailing him, a car that came alongside him, threw open a door and he jumped in—I was thinking in terms of a kidnap. When he returned an hour later he locked himself in his room with his wife. Next morning, he gave me my salary in advance.

A week later he said I have a meeting this evening, so you'll have to stay back. The visitor knows no English. He could have told me that last evening, I thought, but kept quiet. At home there would be disquiet of course. In the afternoon he told me the man's name was Alfonzo Suarez. 'Munitions man.' Very helpful. When would he start talking to me and abandon those staccato sentences he threw around like a cop shooting away because of a nervous trigger finger. By the afternoon he was tinkering with wine glasses, cleaning them and laying the wine bottles. I saw Evelyn walk out and asked her, 'Madam, won't you be here?' She told me not to Madam her ever. 'And what use will I be? You heard him, he speaks only Spanish, the person coming to meet MN.'

Must be a big guy, this Alfonzo. 'They are very formal, these Mexicans,' said MN, 'take an hour just introducing themselves. But please take notes.' A little later, 'You never respond to what I say.' I told him I had nothing to say and so kept quiet.

The man came on time, well-groomed and smelling of aftershave. He greeted Roy a bit pompously detailing some obscure organization he was heading—the 'Organization for the People's Right to Egalitarianism'—something as bombastic and meaningless as that. He also made it a point to say he came from a long line of Spanish nobility, and didn't forget emphasizing that he spoke only Spanish and knew no English. He declined a drink and I giggled since MN had spent an hour laying out his wines. He asked for coffee and I went to the kitchen and got both of them a cup. After some pleasantries MN, who was Senoring him all the while, thought it best to introduce himself, starting with a stab of a tirade against imperialism, and then explaining that he had turned a socialist. 'I thought the good of mankind, which means the proletariat, is a better cause than the good only of Indians.' Alfonzo nodded. Then MN hared off, praising Mexico and the revolution. He started with 1812, and I still had to brush up my history and didn't understand what he was getting at. When he came to 1910, Alfonzo interrupted him politely by putting his hand up.

'1910 was a bit of a fluke senor, I as a Mexican should know. You have obviously heard of Madero—now the revolution itself takes its name from him. He suffered from slight hallucinations, if I may put it that way.'

'Hallucinations?'

'He heard occult voices, Senor Roy, or voices that came from occult sources. If he hadn't heard these voices, he wouldn't have formed the first political opposition in the country. Begging your pardon, I am always a bit suspicious of things occult. In the business that I am in, munitions, we have very little place for such things.' He smiled sardonically as he said this. 'And don't forget he came from a wealthy family. That's why Porfirio Diaz, the previous president, didn't care to crush him immediately.' He paused a bit and added, 'The one who really fouled things up was, of course, the American ambassador.'

'Has to be him, can't be anyone else,' my boss agreed. 'Next only to a British aristocrat, an American diplomat is the most obnoxious you can find anywhere.'

MN had to change the subject, I knew. He did. 'And where would you slot yourself, Senor?' asked MN gently. 'I ask only because we are so many of us on the same side today—communists, syndicalists, anarchists, socialists—that it becomes a bit of a problem to know where each of us stands.'

'I wouldn't want to pigeonhole myself, Senor Roy. If, for an instant, I were to distance myself from my life, the way one leaves a game of chess and looks back at all the moves and counter moves, I'd say I am half socialist with a touch of the anarchist in me. Anarchism lies dormant in my dreams.'

'And what exactly are your dreams about, if I may ask?'

(*A bit impertinent, wasn't he? This kind of conversation should build up slowly, I thought.*)

'Powder and match, bombs and guns.'

'But we have little use for all these here, don't you think?' It wasn't a question, he made it sound as if it was a statement of fact. The guest nodded, sat back and smiled. 'You never know, Senor Roy. Things are fine here, and will remain fine, Dios willing, but you never know. The past has a habit of digging its way up like a rodent sometimes. The old gods are dead but not entombed. Their funeral service has not been held, the Aztec blood still crying out, though we may not hear the cry.'

'I thought the people were quite unified.'

'Suffering over the ages unites people and modernism has bestowed order on the chaos of Latin America in general, it's hidden reality.'

'Aren't we unnecessarily apprehensive? Hidden realities, away from the world's eyes, could turn into unrealities.'

(*Were these people playing games? Why?*)

'To bring back the discussion to our realities, we were talking about what gives muscle to a revolution, weren't we? Probably both. Senor, the game you are playing, or would be playing, you would need them sometime or the other. Philosophy can take you only that far. Revolutions deal more with guns and grenades. Words are just fluff, fake match to fake emotion.'

MN looked hard at Alfonzo. I knew when he became tense he would start tapping his foot, which he was doing at the moment. 'Philosophy is not just words or about words. It is the heart of the struggle, the unseen fire within.'

'Unseen fire remains unseen; what counts, Senor Roy, is the flame that spouts from the barrel at night.'

There was a pause and I got up to serve snacks, and asked him if he would care for wine now. Alfonzo agreed. MN was delighted. He took a childlike delight in showing off his bottles, asking the visitor's preference and then unscrewing the cork.

As he took a sip of the wine, Alfonzo resumed the discussion. 'A big social change as you people desire, means an upheaval, also means bloodletting and sacrifice—sacrificing others as well as yourself—though sacrificing others is always a better option. All is fair on the altar of revolution.'

'Revolutions need to come swiftly, Senor Alfonzo, not on the back of a mule train.'

'I can see in your eyes that you are ambitious.' (He looked at me and said don't translate that.)I translated nonetheless and found MN nodding. 'Exploiters need to be eradicated,' he said, almost without context, 'that's something the revolution does, among other things.'

'Some workers also, isn't it, I refer to eradication?'

'Workers will fight for the revolution, some may die. It is an honour to die for it.'

'Russians would be saying that, wouldn't they, the Lenins and the Trotskys?' He paused for a while and then said, 'Some will die Senor, fighting the upheaval, others resisting it. But the revolution will also kill those fighting for it.' It was Alfonzo nodding away this time.

'A revolution is like a machete in a sugarcane field. It won't be caught discriminating. But you are not specific about your ideology, Senor Alfonzo?'

'Ideology is too big a word for the likes of me. My ideas are an offshoot of my indolence—and family bullying—all the while being told that I was a bum—couldn't manage the workers at the hacienda, labour at the factory. "He will take to drugs one day," said my father to his younger brother in my hearing one day. I was very fond of this uncle, and he of me. I still hold this against my father. So nothing pleased me more than to stay away from my own kind, the rich, if I may use that dirty word, and I am into munitions, and ashamedly rich.'

As he got up to go, he bowed and said, 'Senor Roy, if you ever need arms, for your activities abroad, let me know. I will give them without charge. I will do it for the sake of my scorecard, the card that will be read on the Day of Judgement.' He bowed and left.

Next day, after I had typed out my notes for him to see, MN asked me what I thought of the discussion. I told him at times I thought both of you were playing games. I don't know why he is taken up with you or the revolution, being so rich himself. Guilt, said MN, guilt always has a role to play. And he hates his kind, as he said, I ventured. He shook his head. 'We need to be careful. Did you notice he talked of social change "which you people desire". Significant slip. Hope the Americans didn't send him to me, or the English.'

I didn't dare to contradict him but still managed to say in a half strangled voice—'I thought he was muddled.'

'Affluence, munitions and socialism can't be a happy team. He is muddled all right, as you said, but more so because of his circumstances, they too are muddled. Still we have to be careful.'

Sundays were my own. Ramos would every now and then meet me 'accidentally'. I was reading up on Mexico and would ask questions off Ramos whenever he fell in with me. I remembered about the American ambassador Alfonzo had mentioned. 'Where did you get hold of that?' he asked.I gave an evasive answer.

'It was February 1913, mind you and the former President

Diaz was released from prison by traitors. A right royal battle began between Madero's army and the reactionaries. In a previous election Diaz had got a million votes while Madero, first man to contest an election against him, got 196! Now it was he who was president. Madero blundered choosing General Huerta to lead his troops. For ten tragic days known in Mexico as *La Decena Tragica,* the two sides bombarded each other to pulp. General Huerta had fallen out with Madero, who was a vegetarian and a teetotaller—never drank tequila. Unforgiveable. You can't control Mexico if you live on grass and water, can you? The general was won over by the other side and betrayed Madero. Though I must say there were also those who thought that the General just grew tired of trying to deal with Madero and went over to the other side. The American Ambassador Henry Lane Wilson was more fool than bastard. Of course, like all Americans, he thought he owned Latin America, arranged a meeting between warring generals, appointed Huerta as president—nothing an American ambassador can't do—made the two sides sign such a document in the American embassy. Madero was to be given a safe passage but was shot, along with the vice president, while being transported.'

I let that sink in—always takes time, the enormity of history and revolutions, to turn to sediment within you. He added, 'You know he, Madero, once said, better to die on one's feet than live on one's knees. And in two years he did a lot for the poor.'

Mexico and its eternal revolution were a bit of a puzzle. The country seemed a cauldron with revolutionaries going around as bandits, and bandits going around as revolutionaries. (I used to call them revolutionists, till MN gave me a rap on the knuckles.)One didn't know who was who or which was which. Once you move outside the law, the lines between the two get blurred.The haloes around bandits and revolutionaries were interchangeable, I thought. (When I was silly enough to say this to MN, he shouted at me.) Zapatistas intrigued me. Emiliano Zapata Salazar and Pancho Vila had opposed Porfirio Diaz, the previous president, and Zapata had established and headed the 'Liberation Army of the South', as it was called. After the 1910 revolution,Vila had more or less descended into banditry. But Zapata was a revolutionary at heart, influenced by the anarchist Oaxaca Ricardo Flores Megon. Spaniards have long names. I kept talking of Zapata to Ramos. 'Doesn't he have a base at San Angel?' I asked one Sunday. 'He doesn't,' was the answer.

'There's a monastery there.'

'Yes, but it's not worth your while and it is twenty miles over bad roads or no roads. And Zapata won't be there.'

Zapatistas will, I shot back, insisting on the trip, surely his motorbike could get us there. 'There'll just be ghosts there and nothing else.' When we got there the place looked abandoned, the grass brown and scruffy, and almost no one around. Then we spotted a few peasants who seemed frightened at first, but seeing just two of us, seemed to gather courage and clustered near us, all the while gawking. 'Don't go there,' they said pointing to a rather run-down building, 'there's no one there.' There was. A dozen guys were swinging away, hanged by the Zapatistas I don't know how many days ago; nor would anyone know why. Ropes tied to linter and beam, and the other end knotted around broken necks. The place had a vicious odour. They were peasants swinging there, in rough, threadbare clothes, not hacienda owners. I came out and threw up, and all the way back I had to listen to Ramos reprimanding me for an hour, or so it seemed. I was never going to link Zapata with romance again in my life. The image stored in my mind was of peasants swinging away and the slightly worn out beam holding.

Don't go home just yet, he said to me seeing me depressed, not that he was ebullient either. We went out for a pizza. Sitting over lunch, I just got brave and asked him 'How much of you is Spanish and how much Indian?' Nothing could have been more stupid, but I did ask him. The question had been intriguing me for a while. I was too confused with my own rashness to note his reaction.

'Bold question,' he said, 'but have you any idea what this country, rather, what its people have gone through?' I shook my innocent head.

'I am mixed, though most people can't make out because of the pigment, a factor to be reckoned with both in painting and genetics. A pigment stamps its racial ancestry on you. My mix-up, if I may call it that, started when a Hacienda owner fell in love with an Indian girl and married her, instead of abducting and bedding her. Proper church wedding it was, with many friends of Spanish descent staying away. That was my grandmother, her grandparents, incidentally, who had been properly Christianized.'

'Did your family, or your grandmother's, ever face the Inquisition?'

'Inquisition left us alone, we stood exempted. Both the Franciscan and the Dominican order agreed tacitly to the merging of a Maya or Aztec deity with a Catholic saint; makes life easier for all, isn't it? Please remember though that royal tributes were collected from Indian communities for the expense incurred by Spanish friars to Christianize us—the *encomienda* system as it was called.'

Before we left he said, I want you to remember one thing more. In the sixteenth century, the Indian population with which I identify myself, diminished from thirteen million to two million. Livestock increased, though, he added ironically.

❁

Even stories about him in America were circulated surreptitiously. Here in Mexico, not many people knew about him. Yet his past was consigned to whispers. Where did that arms ship which trawled after him, its hold stuffed with bombs, originate? Java? Sumatra? And the jaws would drop when people heard about his contacts—Rash Bihari, Lala Lajpat Rai! The unfortunates who died for that elephant bomb on the Durbar day, their names had been read out from loudspeakers. Not so our hero. Newspapers couldn't spell his name, AIR had never heard of him it would seem. Talking about him was flashing a mirror message when the sun is overhead.

If actions reveal the man, they did nothing of the sort with him. He wasn't self-conscious, no diffidence about the man who, as rumour went, had never been to college, had taken to bombs and things like water fowl to a lake. His stock had risen with an invitation from the War Minister! There was no change in MN after the meeting, no visible ebullience. The world, or rather, the Mexicans started looking at him in another way. A lesser man may have thrown his chest out a bit, drunk an extra glass of wine, patted friends on the back a bit patronizingly. Not him. It seemed nothing could ruffle him. He was tall and not exceptionally good looking, but he had a presence. You could sense that his thoughts were on the move all the time and in a particular direction. And he was unafraid. When I said this to father he said 'revolutionaries cannot be afraid. Fear gives them a miss.' He, I mean MN had started thawing—you need someone from your country to talk to. He clammed up when I had spoken of people itching to take on the British, father, Harnam Singh, Gobind Bihari, such types. I thought he would lap it up. Instead he looked at me icily and I thought of a double barrelled gun staring at me. For some days I didn't mention the colonial yoke again.

It was not fair on him to have a teenager as secretary. He was considerate, almost compassionate, with me. He was picking up Spanish fast, I noticed a bit fearfully. I can recall some of the things he said. Religion wore a robe of love and carried a sword hidden under the robe, he once said. One was not sure if the robe was initially designed to hide the sword. Original intent and later practice often differed, he added. He was not sure about Russia, where this new state built on Marxism would go, which track it would follow. The planet hadn't seen anything like it, this equality in men; an equality which the state had to force down your throat. How could everyone be equal to everyone?I wondered. But what a good idea!

Once I told him I don't understand what is happening. In fact, many don't. An archduke gets shot and a World War erupts, and then this revolution occurs in Russia. The world is too large, he answered. 'You wake up with an ache in the morning and a stomach bug. You don't know what's happened. Or you get a bad dream—instead of the koh-i-noor you dream of Nadir Shah. You don't know where it came from, the dream. It's the same with reality. One doesn't know which steam pipe will turn cold and which will of a sudden start fizzing, or worse, burst. But let's make the best of what we can comprehend. The feudal armies of Europe are killing each other off, and the feudal structures of Europe are dying, though most of Europe can't see it that way. In Russia the brave Lenin and Trotsky are leading a revolution of workers and peasants. It is a fight against injustice of thousands of years.' I interrupted him. 'You mean a few hundred years, don't you? Since industry came on the scene, coal and cotton.'

'Coal and steam and mining and iron. Don't forget the peasants who have toiled for thousands of years and have to be content with straw and chaff while the grain went to the kulak, landlord, or knight. Well, Lenin and the proletariat are winning; they have to win, if you have any faith in the future. It is the only slab of time which has a flicker of light in it. If you want my views, I would consign the past to hell, or at best to limbo. The present is no better, hence your confusion, but it has a kernel of hope, a seed which may turn into a tree. It's in the future that our promise of paradise lies, the equality which the Jacobins and the guillotine talked of in 1789—Robespierre and Danton, heard of them?' (I nodded.) Reality is too big for any human being to comprehend in its entirety.

I thought to myself that moment that if reality was opaque, unreality was worse, cloaked in a summer dust storm, but I didn't dare open my mouth. Did money have anything to do with this sudden gust of optimism? He had got hold of a hoard of gold coins just after he shifted his residence to the outskirts. He had got hold of an Alsatian dog which he really cared for and loved. He had also bought a rifle and three mouser pistols. Right house in the wrong place with maize fields all around. And what of the Zapatistas and the bandits?

Another day, he was sitting with Evelyn and the two

seemed locked in a serious discussion. They paid no heed to me. It was four in the afternoon and I asked him if I could leave because I saw no work coming my way. I was surprised at his answer. 'I wanted to dictate my article for the El Heraldo de Mexico.' He had begun writing for this journal as well as for Pueblo regularly. Usually he wrote his articles in uneven Spanish, and I smoothened the thing, typed it again and sent it off. I hoped he would be at the job soon, the discussion with Evelyn seemed never ending. I walked over to the balcony but he called me back in. They still seemed to be conferring seriously when I heard him raise his voice ever so slightly and say, 'How long can one move on two tracks, how long? You answer me Evelyn.' Saying this he got up and started dictating to me in English. He always dictated fast, for his brain worked at express speed.

His thoughts tumbling over each other like boulders in an avalanche. As he was nearing the end, I butted in and asked out of the blue, putting my pencil down and laughing, 'What about the two tracks?'

'Oh, you heard that one, did you? You may not understand this just as yet. This is philosophy,' he added jocularly. I plucked up courage. 'A horse has to stick to one track, but you are not a horse. Philosophy need not cramp itself with such restrictions. Evelyn laughed and said, 'What do you think philosophy is?'

'Philosophy is a wild ass. It can cut across tracks, even turn round and do an about turn.' I noticed that the two were stunned.

❁

Superintendent of Police Special Branch of the CID Calcutta, Jeffrey Hughes Denham, had a very successful career dealing with revolutionaries and pseudo revolutionaries. His method had three stages. The first had nothing to do with third degree, he told his colleague Charles Spiegelman, who headed the Crime Branch of the Criminal Investigation Department or the CID, as it was better known. The first stage meant just reasoning with the rebel—don't do it son, you'll regret it. You'll get your freedom when the time is ripe and you Indians know how to handle it. The fellow was even given a chair to sit on, a glass of tea in the lock up, blanket, rice and dal and small steel katori of vegetables. You also dangled that unfailing carrot, money. Turn informer son and you can sleep at home and smoke ganja with your revolutionary cousins. Shout slogans for all you're worth. If that sermon didn't work, the next day when he stood before Denham, the consequences of his actions would be spelled out in no unclear terms—jail and the gallows, and for good measure a rope with the knot in place, would be dangled invitingly in front of him. The third stage was a long one starting with taking off his dhoti, forcing him to lie prone, splashing water on his buttocks and then making one of the burly sepoys take off his rubber shoes and go on a spanking spree. Charles would shake his head in disapproval—he knew of much sweeter methods that went under the pseudonym 'sustained interrogation'. Denham wouldn't budge. 'Charlie, it is the humiliation that does it. They can't stand the shame, especially if the constable comes from the cobbler or the sweeper caste. The sheer indignity of it!'

Charlie wasn't easy to convince, his gospel was bastinado, a few blows on the sole of the feet and back of the knee and a starvation diet to go with it. He laughed, 'Don't give them rice man, and they'll succumb.'

Well, now this unfailing Jeffrey Hughes Denham had been sent to the Americas, first to the States and then to Mexico, to try his hand at getting MN. Blighter finds things different here. You can't put the guy in the cooler, you can't take off his dhoti—not sure if he even wears one, no constables of the tanner or cobbler castes at hand with big-sized tennis shoes! What is the world coming to, Charlie? Relate all this to the boss. And I think we need to be discreet, we're not dealing with Bengali babus here. Every bugger carries a pistol, wears a sombrero and sports a moustache. We want to catch a revolutionary. The Mexicans claim their own revolution is in bloody progress!

The boss was the DIG CID, tough beetroot-red, pipe-smoking hombre from Dorset, which he loved to pronounce as Darzeet. After he had had his three shots of whiskey he would sing,

'There's not a land like Darzeet
Though you'll never come accraaz it
Even if you search through and through
From New Yark to Timbuctoo.'

The boss was not pleased, bosses seldom are. Tell him, he bawled at Charles Spiegelman, 'We are at war damn it and not interested in discretion. Valour is the word. The fellow we have sent him to get is a Bengali babu! He hasn't come from the bloody Andes. What's the bugger talking about! Entire fucking America is behind us and him, so what's his worry? Cold fucking feet, that's what he has got and goosebumps on his damned arse! And he shouldn't call me, I don't wanna talk to him! Understood!'

Charlie understood and relayed the message.

Denham moves in to Hotel Geneva of all places, swarming with Teutons. He goes to the bar, orders a bourbon, and almost spits it out. Never drunk anything so wretched! He chases it with two measures of scotch, just to get the taste out of his mouth. A lady comes in and sits on the bar-stool next to him. The bartender bows and introduces her as the Princess of Bavaria and then discreetly withdraws. Denham of Calcutta CID, true-born Yorkshire man stands up and kisses her hand which he notices smells of cheap perfume.

'And what brings you to Mexico, Herr-Ritter, if I may ask.'

'Business and pleasure, Madame.'

'And what beezness can flawreesh in these time of war Herr…?'

'Denham, I mean…well yes…Denham,' he stammers.

'As I was saying Herr Denham, the awnly beezness that war encourages ees munitions, buy and sell bomb, bullet, torpedo nicht wahr?'

'Not much scope for that, I agree Madame, but I have also come for pleasure, to fish for instance.'

'Feeshing een Mexico city, and not the coast? Very original, and very eenteresting. And if you are meexing beezness with pleasure, may I order a glass of wine for you?'

'No no Madame, it is my privilege to do the honours. Abdar, I mean, bartender, a glass of wine for the Memsab, I mean Princess… Fraulein…?'

'Angelique.' And he says almost audibly to himself, 'Princess! She looks more like a whore.'

'Denken,' she says as the wine glass is placed before her. 'You look a leetle lost, Herr Denham. What are you doing in the evening today?'

'Nothing much, Lady. I will just retire to bed.'

'Bed ees there for better theengs than retiring, Herr Denham, I mean, a good sleep and happy dreams. May I suggest you order dinner in your room. Bartender, dinner for Herr Denham in his room. On my account.'

Barman bows to the Princess of Bavaria, but addresses Denham.

'Sir, shall it be dinner for two?'

'Capital Madame, I mean barman. And obviously on my account.'

'Denken' says the Princess, as she goes into his room when the dinner is served and asks, 'I don't see your feeshing tackle, fly, rod.' I could leave them there but I won't. After some more whiskies and wine and jousting in bed, she keeps up with her affected French accent and asks, ' if you haven't come feeshing for fish, what have you come feeshing for, liebling?'

He laughs and finds he can't control his laughter, has had too much to drink. 'You are asking a very loaded question, luv.'

'Loaded did you say liebling? I have a good friend who deals in munitions. I must introduce him to you tomorrow. Good Mexican can be of great help to you. He will find the feesh you want to fry!'

'I just want to fry a Bengali.' Denham almost chokes with laughter, and she gives him water to drink and slaps him on the back.

It all unravels later, a bit through the efforts of Ramos, a bit through the Germans who almost beat up the 'Bavarian princess'. The damage had been done. She was also drunk and forgot in the morning what she had prized out of Denham at night! Even if the great Kaiser Wilhelm was on the back foot now, and war was getting over with soldiers on both sides leaving the trenches to the rats, you couldn't have a Teutonic version, however poor of Mata Hari bringing such a bad name to both those noble professions, spying and whoring. Unforgiveable! Yet Angelique remembered the word he had used—loading, and Alfonzo during his tryst with Angelique got scent of it and made a beeline for Denham. It was the bartender who came to our rescue—it was him that Ramos contacted. The fellow listened in, and his version went as follows:

Denham immediately sensed that the munitions man was after a sucker and who better that an English sucker from Calcutta? He played along. For the first half hour there was hardly any talk between the two—Alfonzo didn't speak English. He phoned up his office to send an English speaking person. So, initially, the barman was functioning as interpreter and translator. The negotiations started the moment the English speaking girl from Alfonzo's office arrived.

'Senor, if we need munitions, it would be for the European theatre where we are already winning. There's, of course, Turkey you know, Gallipoli and all that shit. Surely we wouldn't need supplies from Mexico for a war raging on the Bosporus, don't you think?'

'Then why did Senor come all the way to Mexico? A shepherd seeks pastures close to his sheep.' I fancied that this little speech was capped by a sardonic smile.

'In war, you grab things from wherever even the moon is not too far, ha ha.'

'My ordnance is nowhere near the moon senor. It is at your service.'

They get into a huddle, and the bartender loses the thread.

Head a-split with a hangover, Denham nevertheless knows what he has to do. He shambles into the American Embassy and asks to meet the consular officer. He is made to sit in a quiet room. After a few minutes an American officer comes in and asks politely, 'Thank you for coming, Mr Jeffrey Hughes Denham, we've been expecting you.'

He is surprised they know his full name, because his card just read J.H. Denham. They shake hands and the American asks, 'What can we do for you?'

He rambles about terrorism, bombs, Calcutta-Cologne and Bengali-German conspiracies not just against the empire but targeting Anglo-American friendship. The American listens gravely and then eventually asks, 'What exactly do you have in mind?'

'There are two avenues, if I may venture to suggest. The first choice would be to take him back and thus prize out details of other conspirators, bomb makers etc., you understand?'

'Through force?'

'Yes, of course, old man, you can't get by in this game without some force, isn't it, a tickle in the ribs here and a prod in the arse there?'

'Kidnapping happens to be a criminal offence all over the world, Mr Denham. And what is the other option you were thinking of exploring?'

'Well, there's a word called "elimination", isn't there?'

'With respect, Mr Denham, considering our very delicate relations with Mexico at this instant, I am afraid both avenues you suggested are closed.'

Denham gets the impression that he is being treated like a WOG just because he is tanned after twenty years in the wretched sun of Hindustan. So, the buggers are not prepared to bend rules, is it? They didn't even offer me a cup of coffee! Would have helped me with this headache. I'll show them! He proceeds to the French Embassy. Pour quoi they say, why come to us? Still struggling with his hangover and the effects of the de riguer jousts with Angelique, he tells them about this terrible terrorist from India. They produce an officer who was previously with the French Foreign Legion, blue patrols and handlebar moustaches. Man after my own heart, cries Denham, when he sees him. 'Monsieur, I have sabred many a bastard in the black lands, I mean bad lands of Africa. I am the man you are looking for and you are the man I am looking for. There's no adventure in this place unless you are a Pancho Villa or Zapata.'

The next morning MN's dog, which he loved, dies. Ramos thinks he has been poisoned, it's now time to tell MN about the plot against him. The Germans are phoning up regularly as it is and keeping Ramos informed.

It's the first MN hears of CID Superintendent Denham. He doesn't seem to be worried. Business as usual, but he does take a round and surveys the surrounding maize fields and beyond it the wild growth of cactus and shrub. In the evening, a ramshackle truck comes up. Four or five locals with spade and shovel lean out. It halts near the house. What on earth for?

They get down and start scything the wild growth around the house. 'Rather late in the day,' says MN. 'They should have been here in the morning, isn't it?' Ramos thinks nothing of it and sits on his motor cycle and buzzes off home, but I stop him and insist he leaves his pistol with me, never know what may happen in the night, if the Germans are to be believed. Then a car rolls down and we see a tall man, dressed in blue patrols, his head shaven, his eyes piercing blue, get down. He looks like a general, in fact, a field marshal. A tanned fellow is sitting with him. Immediately, the ones who were cutting down the wild plants leap up and rush with spade and crowbar into the house. I hear gunshots, seem to be coming from the same weapon, I can make out the spatter of lead against the wall. I want to run to MN's defense but my legs refuse to move. I now check if the pistol is loaded, look at the sky and let go, thank God there's no plane overflying MN's house at that moment. The local toughs are stopped in their tracks, but one huge guy manages to penetrate to MN's bedroom where he is calmly sipping scotch with his left hand and holding a pistol in his right. The fellow retreats in haste and encounters me, but all the six bullets from my, or rather Ramos' Smith and Wesson, are already in the Mexican sky. I still point my pistol at him but he calls my bluff, lifts me and runs to the car. It is then I hear the man in Blue Patrols sneering at the tanned guy sitting with him. 'Did you bring me for this monsieur to kidnap a beautiful lady! I have honour on my side, I am from the French Foreign Legion!' And he points the pistol towards Denham and shoots him, before he shoots the hulk who was almost making off with me.

❁

A journal is a recollection, and recollections have their own problems especially when events seem to be scrimmaging with each other. Writing now in the first person of a time when I had just stepped out of my teens, confronting a new culture in a new country, slightly suspicious of the only 'friend' I seemed to have, suspicious of his intentions, hoping Ramos wouldn't fall in love with me, knowing that such a suspicion was most presumptuous; managing a difficult boss with a wife who was cordial but aloof, a boss who was miles above me in intellect and experience, and was aware of it, and at times made me aware of it—it is all a bit tough putting it down coherently in a journal. Events…did I mention events? Well, they were gathering like flies around sweets in India. Success was slowly coming his way, like-minded people from the left quietly clustering around him, getting pally with left-leaning Americans who had skipped over to Mexico to escape going to war in Europe. Mexico must have been paradise compared to the trenches. Must look up details of the war.

Were the Yankees ever in Somme—I know it was the Aussies in Gallipoli. But I was talking of MN and his ascendant star. The culmination of it all was a meeting with the president, General Don Venustiano Carranza himself.

There were also the Indian 'revolutionaries' and most came for money. How is it we Indians of whatever ilk can smell money across sea and savannah and then manage to swoop like buzzards on a kill? Which of the senses plays a part here? Some of them, the desi revolutionaries, after taking money from him, asked me where MN got the coins from, they were gold coins, mind you, though he had exchanged some of the money for American dollar bills. They knew the money came from Germany, but still they asked, where's the harm in a question? Their audacity was unbelievable. When I told him about some of the things these revolutionaries said, he just laughed it off. 'Don't let it worry your little head,' he said, ruffling my hair gently. He was generous—would part with a thousand or more dollars without any problem. How long would his treasure trove last? Having lost the war, the Germans had started leaving Mexico.

We had no such trouble with Mexicans or the disenchanted Americanos, whose disenchantment was with the trenches—which they had never been to—that was a different matter. One couldn't help overhearing conversations. How people attacked the state! In the eyes of some of the Mexicans, the villain was the state and its main role was to defend private property, and the dirtiest word in their vocabulary was a 'status quo-ist'. MN was fond of grouping such people as Anarcho-Syndicalists. Since there was not enough work for me in the office, now that he had picked up Spanish—I started studying Marx and whatever communist literature I could lay my hands on. I noticed it impressed MN, though the wife was impervious to my efforts at learning. He had, of course, no time for me. Firstly it was a full house—Evelyn, Maria, the cook (I thought she was even more good-looking than the wife), and the visitors. The houses, both at Colonia Roma and the one he had shifted to, were the tramping grounds for Mexican socialism; in and out they went, faces radiant with expectation (of what?), thumping of chests and hail Bolshevism—whatever that may mean—written all over their faces. And then the Bolshevik came home!

For MN and his socialist cronies it was as if Jesus had dropped from the cross (on furlough from Calvary) and walked across to drop his calling card on us. 'I am Jesus from Nazareth (it's in Palestine, friend), sorry am a bit sozzled, I mean I am a Lenin crony from Mouscova actually. Pleased to meet ya, revolutionary comrade. You're the one who started the first communist party in the world outside Russia, aren't you? Hope you're well stocked with dough.' I am being both facetious and spiteful—must admit I resented him initially, the space around MN was getting crowded. He had many names, I was to discover, Brantwein, Borodin—his real name, and a name for America! He even had a family under a false name, the wife never knowing his real identity. He was suave, his bearing aristocratic, from the little I knew of the Russians, I felt he was more a Czarist than a Bolshevik. Needless to say, he was more gracious with Maria than with me—after all she managed the household and cooked fabulously. The palate often determines which way a friendship lies. She was Mexican and I was Indian; that also counts. Actually, no one in the house had time for me except when I was needed on the Olivetti or when something really important had to be drafted in Spanish. MN told me once how he had been complimented on his Spanish because of something I had drafted. Possibly I may have simply improved his draft, who cares? 'Did you tell whoever about me?' I asked a little self-consciously and a little stupidly. He just smiled and didn't answer.

I saw him typing one morning and asked if I could help; he waved me away, didn't want me near him or look at what he was typing. I kept away, not a very difficult thing to do, and yet difficult. Why was he keeping something from me? What was so important that he had to keep it to himself? I was a nobody. How would my knowing something affect anything or anybody? Evelyn came and overlooked the typing which made me more jealous. What had I to do with it? He even had a carbon paper on and as he finished, Evelyn asked why the hell do you need a copy? She crumpled it along with the dark blue thoroughly indented carbon paper and threw it in the bin. That evening I did a sneaky thing, a bit, only a bit, ashamed of it. I picked the crumpled copy up, went home and read it carefully.

Yes, he had no time for me but there were days when he was alone, this was before the Russian made his entry. Evelyn had gone out to a library. Father had been talking to me of the Irish rebellion at Easter. Thakur Brajbir Singh had kept his ears close to the ground and had talked also of an anti-British agitation at a place called Champaran in Bihar. MN was alone that day in the house and I asked him what he thought of all this. I remember his answer, words coming out with difficulty through pursed lips. 'These are puffs of smoke on the horizon. The real fire on the skyline is the Bolshevik Revolution. Who told you about Champaran?'

'Father.'

'Hmm, India gets into the bone with us Indians…as it should,' he added hastily.

'Has it got into your bones?' I marvel at my audacity now. 'You are very bold,' he said, not too happily. He got busy with his books, and then came back to my table to ask, 'What have you noticed that you asked me that question?'

'You don't speak much about India…it is all Bolsheviks and Mensheviks.' He nodded, 'Not enough, I agree.'

'Why?'

'Because there are bigger things to worry about, a revolution that can change the way humanity has lived till now. It will end the exploitation of the poor, worker and peasant.'

'But they are being exploited in India as well.'

'You don't understand. Firstly, there are hardly any workers in India, we are not industrialized. I am referring to the planet. Lenin is talking of humankind.'

When you are locked out of conversations, you learn to listen. I found conversations were veering a bit away from Lenin and Trotsky to Marx and someone called Hegel. I knew of Marx and was reading up on him, but Hegel remained distant. I soaked in words like 'petit- bourgeois-reformist' and the like and soon noticed that 'anti-imperialist' was no longer in much use. A lone word can always tell you as much as a story.

Autumn 1919, the leaves on the trees turned crinkled amber rather than gold. The voices in the house became muted when I was around, there was more whispering. I kept away, who was I to pry and for what good reason? The scene had changed and suddenly become more surreptitious. When things are moving into a shadow you can never tell when they will emerge into light? Does darkness provide the right ambience for conjectures? What happens to people when a fuse blows and the lights go out? What happens when a woman is suddenly woken up by a rumble in the attic or a scurry of rat legs under the floorboards? She dare not even leave the bed, all the while praying that the sounds stop and the night returns to its silence. I am dramatizing. When you don't know what's happening, the best you can do is to turn to drama. Well, suddenly conversations turned to whispers—*phus-phus* was the word in India. I came one wintry Monday to find the house locked. Where had everyone gone? And without saying a word to me? A short holiday perhaps, but they would have told me. How could this happen? That week I haunted the house, waiting and often walking through the reeds on the periphery. Word must have gotten out on my prowling for one morning I saw a socialist whom I used to see with MN, was waiting for me. He was very polite, as Mexicans are, and took me to a restaurant for coffee, and there handed me an envelope which bore my name in his handwriting. He cautioned me not to open it right there. When I left he said, don't talk about him and don't make enquiries. A disappearance such as this has its own rules around it.

I kept feeling the thick envelope from time to time as I walked back, and each time I did this my heart sank. I went home and mother was fortunately in the kitchen for I wanted to be alone. I already knew its contents by touch, but hoped there was a letter for me. There wasn't. All it contained was dollar bills—three months' salary. Not a word or a line, not even an *au revoir.* I cried putting a pillow over my head so that mother wouldn't hear me sobbing.

The Tense Years

He had gone off to Berlin and Moscow via numerous places—with false passports. If the victors of the war are on your tail, your passage had better be sinuous. Everything was secret—passage, destination, and the name he went under—and, of course, all of it kept from me, all this can get under your skin when you are young. Two months later, Ramos had filled me in, even on these details.

What is the point of a journal if the bare skeletal truth is not laid down? Yet, how can I compress in a few pages those years of brooding. He had gone to Germany and Russia at the tail end of the War and the start of a bloody revolution. Lives did not matter, doctrine did, while for the other side shooting revolutionaries was like swatting flies. The regime's doctrine sinks into the gendarmerie and the police. They think killing is the right thing to do. In fact, it is the only course left open. Revolutionaries think likewise, and so it goes on, kill and counter-kill, each snug within his own borders. To distract myself, I burrowed into Marx and Engels, even read what Marx had to say about the mutiny, our own 1857. But my mind was fixed on Berlin and Moscow, wherever MN was, right in the burning coals. News from the blood-flecked zones was sketchy and one didn't know whether to believe the American press which borrowed from the British press (I was not *au fait* with the expression 'Fleet Street' then).

Father was in touch with someone in California. I noticed the letters were post-marked USA. There were calls from California as well. He had confided in mother but hadn't talked to me. (I seemed to be left out everywhere.) One afternoon with both sitting formally, Balbir had been kept out of the room, I was called in and told we could be shifting to California. You know what the formality reminded me of, Seema? This is how daughters were told by their parents about whom she would be marrying shortly—everything arranged, token money given, husband to be was short and on the darker side but so what beti, you are not exactly the sun, are you now? All I could say was what about the police, hope they won't be after you. Everything has been taken care of. I am not on the police records. Nothing is keeping you now in Mexico, is it Shail? I shook my head, nothing was keeping me here now. As we got up, and I saw Balbir disappearing from the door (he was eavesdropping, the rascal), I asked father who was the angel in California who had fixed all this? Gurdeep Singh, he said, brother of Harnam Singh. Sikhs, he added, you won't find anyone more loyal.

He was wrong about the police. Six months or possibly a year after we landed in California, regular passport and visa, no hanky panky, the police knocked at our door, just one man in blue. Once he was seated he said, 'Mr Rathore, one of our senior consular officers has come down to have a word with your daughter. You could, of course, accompany her.' He knew nothing of why anyone would want to meet me. Father had no option but to agree. The meeting was fixed for Tuesday next and father drove me to the police station from where we were taken to a nice isolated house and seated in a lobby. Within minutes an officer in a suit and a lady walked in. The officer was a tall man with a slight stoop, and looking down half the time as tall people tend to do. He gave his name as Markham. His smile did not appear very warm. Somehow I thought the face and the profile looked a wee bit familiar. Where could I have seen him? The lady was warmer and said she was Ms Susan Foster. The lady did ask us how we were faring in California and wasn't it a good change from Mexico and then Markham opened up.

'Miss Rathore, we would have preferred talking to you alone, but knowing Indian fathers and husbands, we did not want to worry your family unduly. Am I right, Mr Rathore?' Father duly nodded his head and said Markham was very right. 'We would be very happy if you answered us frankly. This, of course, is going to be a one-to-one conversation and strictly confidential. You can see that your police escort is out of earshot.' He was interrupted by a man entering and saying to father, 'Mr Rathore, there is a call for you' and took him away. 'As I was saying, we know something about the man you worked for in Mexico. Some of us from the consular service treat him as dangerous. Personally, I would consider him interesting.' Father came back carrying a cup of tea with a cookie sticking out of the saucer. Markham raised an eyebrow. The lady, Ms Foster, gave a friendly smile though.

Markham was still waiting for me to say something. 'I don't fully understand what you want me to say. Yes, I worked as a secretary to Mr MN, but how would that interest you? You would know everything about how he organized the communist party in Mexico, I believe the first outside Russia.'

'Now we call it Soviet Russia,' Ms Foster said kindly. I

didn't mind her at all. 'But now he has gone to Moscow. A lot of things are taking place in Europe—wars, revolutions, new philosophies taking over nations, new parties one had never heard of. We are interested in Europe, we fought there as well. We are told that money has been abolished in Soviet Russia. So, how is day-to-day living transacted? I buy a quart of milk by giving the milkman two eggs, is that how the market is run? Others tell us there is nothing in the market to buy or sell. They are close to famine because peasants are producing only enough for their own subsistence. They won't want to give the surplus to the state?'

I answered, 'I read what anyone would, sitting here, all that comes in the press. I have no particular access to anything happening in Russia or Germany or in any country in Europe.' Markham took up where Susan Foster had left. 'The German ambassador, Mirbach, was killed in his office by a Russian socialist desperado. There was a time but a year-and-a-half ago when we were told that the revolution was moving from Germany to Russia. Germany has even withdrawn its embassy from Russia now, the least they could do if their ambassador was assassinated. We have no idea what type of country we would be dealing with? To come to other issues, as his secretary you were quite close to him, the one you refer to as MN. People are known to confide more in their secretaries than in their wives.'

Father interrupted here. 'This would be the case with old secretaries, not with someone like Shail, who was looked upon more as an apprentice.'

Ms Foster asked, 'Has there been no communication from him so far?'

'None.'

'Do you expect us to believe that?'

'If there was, you would have known, you'd have intercepted the letter.' I look back and am still a bit surprised how I could be that bold. 'I wasn't even privy to his plan of escape and details about his journey to Germany and then to Moscow.'

'You knew he was going to Berlin first?'

'Much after he left. I came to know this from the socialists in Mexico after he left.'

'Was it the munitions man?'

I was startled, shaken. 'Who? No, I don't know any munitions man.' I was trying to think desperately.

'You made notes Ms Rathore, during a meeting between him and MN. He thought your word counted for much. That is why it is hard to believe that you are completely out of touch now. And may I mention here that our country did you a good turn. There was a certain CID officer from Calcutta who wanted our help in kidnapping this icon of yours and take him back to India. We gave a curt no to the project.'

Susan Foster intervened. 'You need to be beholden to Mr Markham, for he was the one who said no to the British officer.'

'The drunk officer weighed down by a stupefying hangover,' said Markham with a wry smile. 'Must have got a gallon of beer down his throat the previous night.'

'But he got us where he wanted, almost.'

'Almost, Miss Rathore, but with French help I believe. Hope you are glad nothing serious happened.'

I did tell them though that MN was no longer an Indian revolutionary, and when they asked what I meant by that, I told them that he was no longer interested in the freedom struggle for India. His outlook had turned global. He thinks that the Bolshevik revolution was the greatest thing that had happened to humankind. He was no longer interested in bombs and that sort of thing, getting a shipload of German arms to India and setting off an insurrection. You could tell that to your English friends, and I smiled. He nodded. Some tea came in for us as well, and sandwiches. But Markham was not the man to let go. 'We notice you are borrowing a lot of books on communism, and I don't just mean Marx. So, you have been bitten by the Marxist bug? You could become an expert on the subject one day, you know. It could stand you in good stead. When things settle down there, and they will settle down, that's the law of political upheavals, you can't have stormy weather eternally, storms can't be the norm, nor can revolutions. Am getting long-winded sorry, you could even think of a trip to the kremlin, why not? Odd things are happening. We can't make head or tail of some of the things taking place there. We are told the workers have raided the cellars of the rich—they call them the bourgeoisie—but instead of drinking the liquor and getting sozzled they break the bottles—all that expensive liquor going down the drain breaks my heart, Ms Rathore. I believe in one of the houses witnesses beheld fountains of champagne going waste. They could have sold the liquor to us—we'd have given them dollars!'

There was much laughter. Then Mr Markham turned serious.

'They have set up a secret police, a commission as they call it to combat counter-revolution and sabotage. And it is under a Polish ideologue, Dzerzhinsky.'

'Iron Felix, you mean?' He looked at me hard, his expression almost articulate, where had this girl picked up this nugget? 'He is said to be austere and, of course, a fanatic. Bad combination. I don't trust such people. Crooks are easier to handle.'

A little while later, I followed this up by saying that he lived like any of his soldiers, no gratification of the senses, the simplest food. But there was that statement of his where he said, 'We stand for organized terror…terror is an absolute necessity in times of revolution'. I reminded Markham what he had said. 'We judge quickly. In most cases, only a day passes between the apprehension of the criminal and his sentence. When confronted with evidence criminals, in almost every case, confess. And what argument can have greater weight than a criminal's own confession? I had learnt that eight hundred had been shot without trial near the Winter Palace. A mass of undigested rumours is brought to him and he decides. And I got carried away.' The Poles were much earlier on the revolution wagon than the Russians. Their Polish Proletariat Party was set up in 1882, twenty years ahead of the Russian soviets. And Rosa Luxemburg was Polish, slaughtered in 1919 by the German Horse Guards. They were a bit taken aback, Markham and the elegant lady.

They had other questions, of course. Who is Lenin's Number 2, is it Zinoviev or Trotsky? This made me laugh, who has the gumption to call him by his first name, Ilyitch? I guessed that their Menshevik sources had told them all sorts of things.

He got up, and so did Foster. 'You should meet our experts on the Left one day. It will soon develop into an industry. The rest of the world doesn't want revolutions, you can bet. Even the peasantry want routine, life should run as it always has. They went through war and the Germans got the better of them. They have abolished money you know, and soon hunger will get the better of them. And three revolutions in one year—February to October. Our experts don't know who fired the first shot—was it men or philosophies? They'd be glad to exchange notes. Yes, and any interesting thoughts on the Cheka?'

'It will turn into the sword-arm of the revolution, Mr Markham. It will do what the guillotine did in France.'

We have all grown old. Regret is at the centre of old age. He never got his due, MN. India didn't bother about him, and the Russians, I mean the post-revolution Russians forgot him he had to flee Moscow like some hunted counter revolutionary; I am using the worst word in our language, communist language, where rapists and murderers would be considered decent folk compared to a counter-revolutionary. I think China did him in, and it was not his fault but the blinkered thinking of the Comintern, its ambiguous policy, for it wanted to set the East afire, but how? Through the Kuomintang of Chiang Kai-shek which Soviet Russia was arming? When MN was deputed to China, Borodin was already there. The Kuomintang had many landlords in its ranks. How could one think of an agrarian revolution and the peasants seizing the land they had cultivated? Stalin was clever, he asked the Chinese communists to seize the land as also collaborate with the Kuomintang. The landowners with Chiang Kai-shek were not going to stand for this and massacred twenty-seven thousand communists in Canton.

What could they do? The Russians were trying to bring about a Chinese revolution through the Kuomintang initially. These two were the implementers. Communists were advised to seize the land as well as collaborate with the Kuomintang.

If you seize the swamp, you can't at the same time collaborate with the crocodile. Any Indian peasant could have told them that.

No poem has ever been written on his heroic return, the traverse over the stark freezing Gobi Desert, can you imagine, crossing the Gobi desert! Has any Indian leader done a tenth of what he did?

He fell from grace—Stalin wouldn't meet him. His downfall started from China and the betrayal by Kuomintang.

Note: Seema, I am adding a little note for you on the Revolution. It is one of the greatest events that have taken place in the world. Please note I speak in the present tense. The Revolution will always be with us. People will tell you that just as oligarchies ruled the countries the world over, so did the communist minority rule over proletariat and peasantry. A minority always has to rule, the mass can't rule by itself. But it is the stir among the masses that brings about a revolution. Never lose faith in October 1917.

[End of journal]

That's where mother had come to a halt. She was not the dramatic type. Drama was my forte. Yet, she had left the journal hanging in there with the Cheka and the notional guillotine. The guillotine of 1789–1790 was like St Francis of Assisi compared to Stalin's firing squads. It took me some time to absorb the packed details of the journal. I had very little idea of Komagata Maru. And as for Mexico, had just read a chapter somewhere on Montezuma and his innocent faith in the word of the invaders from the old world. Of course the old civilized world never forgot to tell you about the human sacrifices of the Aztecs, skull murals adorning the outer walls. Was always told by mother that Cortes was a *harami*. Does youth mean ignorance? I started wondering on these lines. And does age imply memoirs despite memory loss, weakness in the joints and a bladder out of control? Is that all that can be said for old age? Am I guilty of over-simplification?

You clammed up Mama, but I am reading up on the man, have precious little else to do. Information then must have been scanty, but now it is freely available. His glory days were all in the twenties, meeting Lenin, on first name basis with Zinoviev—the then number two to Lenin, friends with the greatest communists from the world over. I am just trying to imagine what it must have been like, a near famished peasantry, but spirits soaring in Petrograd and Moscow, the young people feeling as if utopia and heaven were within reach. MN meets the greatest in the left world, John Reed the biggest communist of America, hears the son of John Connolly, the iconic hero of Ireland. Have heard of the father, Mama, the one who led the Easter Rebellion in Dublin against England, the one with the shattered leg, brought on a stretcher to be shot after the rebellion was crushed. Wonder if there were any trials, they were all shot within a fortnight, the Easter rebels. That was British justice those days. So, why are we all crying foul when Stalin resorted to the firing squad? Zinoviev, Bukharin, Borodin, MN's friend, the one who fetched him from Mexico, the one who was with him in China. Except that Stalin had over a million killed. But the Revolution was like a flame, they would have loved to die for it. They were the ones who swarmed Moscow, hope and aspiration outstripping reality, ignoring it, fiery words with nothing to sustain the fire. Marx, had he been living, would have been both happy and worried in November 1917.

Mama I am overawed, reading your journal gives me goosebumps. What a life, moving from land to land, farm outback to Canada, Mexico and then California! Not outback really, you were, as we Indians say, 'on the backside' of Lucknow, close to Chinhat, weren't you? I can see behind the word Mama, I can spot you as my eye overruns the lines. A daughter doesn't have to be present to imbibe, intuit a mother's past. This gift comes from the placenta, this sense of being there in your past, without being there. I am making sense to myself, though am not sure if it would have appealed to you, were you alive. As I end your journal I feel your heart was not in Canada or Mexico or wherever but in Moscow. I could be wrong. You felt the thrill of those moments, utopia dawning on a smoke-filled, destitute world, Russian soldiers shambling back in torn boots and ragged clothes, with nothing in the belly except hunger.

I can sense your edginess, you wanted to be there and were not there, cold, starved Moscow where the knights of the Revolution were holding out against exploiters, Kulaks, imperialists, the white counter-revolutionists. (Some of the white soldiers were still on horseback, weren't they?) A bit apocalyptic, don't you think? For how many months did Stalin hold out, at Tsaritsyn, that was what this port on the Volga River was called no? The white Russians took it till Stalin and Vorshilove attacked again and drove them off in January 1920. Five years later it became Stalingrad.

Trotsky, Bukharin—they must have looked like apostles to you. Lenin as Jesus, of course. Don't know where to place the early Stalin, tough guy, MN says he went through major surgery without anaesthesia. The amazing thing is the combination of hunger and euphoria, hand in hand, descending on the proletariat. I am unable to think of Camelot having never read about Arthur and his round table. The only round table I know of is that of George V and Gandhi in chappals and dhoti and stick. Had Gandhi been in a suit, no one would have remembered that round table. His name hardly figures in your journal, but never mind. I admire your tenacity Mama,you didn't waver once you took the plunge. There were no easy political fords you crossed. You stuck to Marx. That's saying a lot, to stick to Marx. I was told by an old comrade that sticking to Marx was sticking to Stalin. His word was law to the Indian communist. The Yezov terror killed millions, and the leaders the Bukharins and Zinovievs and others were brought down like skittles. Mama, no matter what your hero may have thought of Lenin, and am certain you would have felt the same if you had gone on with the journal, don't forget he brought in the Cheka, misnamed as the 'Russian Extraordinary Commission for Combatting Counter Revolution and Sabotage', which sounded more like an essay than a title.

And Mama, whatever you may say, the Tsar was not so unpopular. When he was dethroned, a church was full of crying peasants who started wailing 'now what will become of us?' You will say this is Western propaganda, am not so sure. The Tsar was the master (*Khozian*) of the Russian land. And while they cried, they also kissed each other in jubilation at his fall, and they wore their best dresses to the church to celebrate. Religious processions were taken out to thank the Lord. The people, especially the peasantry, are basically moved by contrary impulses. The peasants actually thought that since they would be voting, the Constituent Assembly would be one of peasants *(Muzhitskim)*. Had they known that they would never be at the table, that the peasantry will plough, and it's the others—the ones with degree and pedigree—who will decide what's to become of the state and society (which means the peasantry too) and literature, and the church, and why leave God out of it, they'll decide what happens to God too, which dark crypt, black with candle soot, to put him in.

Wish I could have asked you, was it a revolution? Revolutions are supposed to be sudden, aren't they like a bomb going off? No, not the right analogy. Revolutions start with mobs in the streets, sticks and stones and a few catapults, and the gendarmerie fires on them, resulting in absolute slaughter. Then more mobs, mob rule, anarchy and then dictatorship. This one had a long fuse, since the assassination of Alexander II, that was over thirty years back, on the day he was to accede to further liberal measures—he had already abolished serfdom. The moment you turn liberal, after a long night of tyranny—say two centuries long—a bullet gets inserted in some chamber with your name on it. But surely, 1905 was the thing. Anyone could have foretold that it was on its way, a revolution, right since the wintry night when the unarmed hymn-chanting mob was fired upon at the Winter Palace. A peasant's union was formed, and the first thing it did was to ask for the abolition of private property. But why am I going on and on about the past? For you, 1917 would defy the past tense, would remain ever present, something almost palpable, a part of you. Was it January 26, when the Tsar ordered the troops to fire on a mob? I am reading up on the Rev. Mama, April and Lenin returns from Switzerland in a special train provided by the Germans. And land gets nationalized! I find it hard to believe. Your father, Thakur Brajbir Singh, would never have gone along with that, would he? Indira nationalized banks, Lenin nationalized land! And the land must have been three times the size of India. Forgive my errors if I have committed any, I sure don't wish to be a historian of the Russian Revolution.

Mama, my moods change. Please don't talk of revolutions. People want bread not Bukharin, and a little liquor after a hard day near the factory boiler rather than Lenin. Ideologues don't realize this, nor do those who lead revolutions.

Mama, am not going to ask you where you or your hero fit into all this. What's the point? I picked up a book on Stalin the other day at a book shop and looked up the index. There wasn't a line on MN Roy, not one word. Browsed through a book on Bukharin, looked up the index again, not a line wasted on your hero. Can history also be so fickle? If he wasn't Bengal-brown, would he have been treated this way? The Polish lady, Rosa Luxemburg, battered to death, figures everywhere, she remains an icon. Silly thoughts, need to be disregarded. But all was forgotten, his failed heroics in China, snuffed out by the Chiang Kai-shek treachery.

I am getting up from the wrong side of the bed these days, and each time that happens, I have a new take on your journal. Don't talk to me of revolutions Mama, don't talk of revolutions. People don't want them—all they want is a cooking fire and bread, naan or roti and something to go with it, onion or pickle or chick peas, water that is clean, a glass of clear water through which the mother can see her child's face, a roof, thatch, tile whatever, and if the times are kind, a set of walls to go with it. Am talking of the poor Mama, as for the rich, they'd need another planet to devour, a planet loaded with at least silver, gold being out of reach, silver *bhi chalega,* and some French cuisine—lamb marinated in Bordeaux, beef in red wine or sherry and a sprig of basil and a pinch of thyme; also a bag in which she could keep her ego, bag made of the hide of a female ibex; and for the male, a ruby stud flashing from the mistress's nose, and—there's a whole planet to eat off and drink off damn it, and then walk as if the planet belonged to you, and it does, it does, it belongs to the rich, legacy from God on high.

A week later, I take up your journal and I have a completely different take on it. How staid you were when you wrote this, as if you were writing about some other person, as if you were dealing with one of the numerous wives of Gilgamesh, disembodied you chronicling a Babylonian queen. Not a dream did you touch, a night dream turning into an anxiety, something tangible for a while floating from one corner of the ceiling to another with the accompaniment of background music—rat legs scurrying somewhere. And you drew back from the end. It wasn't just blood and gore and Dracula that you sidestepped, you just shut out the end, which didn't have just one villain but two, and one of them was Edgar Hoover.

We don't get the sludge of everyday living from the journal, it is words and more words, dark centipedes on a white sheet, they are history not biography of a life lived with its light and laughter, its smells, the overhang of gasoline fumes and CO2. I've a feeling that if you were not in Vancouver or in Mexico but in Chicago, the journal would not have smelt meat or the smoke from gangland guns, and at least a whiff of Al Capone vanishing like the Devil on a lambent evening after a tryst with Doctor Faustus.

The Letters

Have been reading your letters, Mama. You see, a month back I decided to open the locker in the bank. You always told me there was no money in it. And there wasn't, except for fifteen thousand rupees kept in an envelope, in grandmother's handwriting. That's what she had left you. Picked up a silver chain with a sapphire pendant. You had told me the story. Dad had got the pendant from his mother, but couldn't buy a gold chain, so he had it fixed on a silver one and gave it to you. Oh, the toils of being communist! But, there were the letters!

You'll permit me to philosophize Mama, I hope. Someone should write your biography one day, but am not sure what all will get in and what will be left out. It is your disillusion that troubles me. To end with disillusion for something you have worked for all your life is a bit baffling. But you stepped away from rejection. Have started wondering about people who are still alive and kicking, reading their biographies. It will be just that swatch of politics which will show in the life of a politico, elections won and lost, parties changed (no mention of barter money) and of course none of the mistresses will be named, and if it's a woman politician, then the studs in khadi. If one is writing about Mata Hari, it will just be her affairs and espionage. What about fits of anger and spasms of regret and interludes of love? What of a bad dream that turns your morning tea bitter and you don't want to even touch the paper, what of failure and dejection, looking back and ruminating on destiny and how one has drifted, for we drift like a fallen leaf in the wind, we need to respect the scratch and scrape of a dry leaf as it moves with a halo of dust around it, dust and leaf propelled by the wind, like sisters drifting into marriage; a night of love kept away from the world's eyes; the fear of acne, the guilt of squeezing a pimple; and distractions—even memory and thought are distractions, you sit down to write and think of the face of the editor, or the smell that comes from the mouth of the sub sitting in the same cubicle as you; the gallop of blood in anger or in lust; the lighting of an incense stick, the pouring of milk in the dog's bowl, or the terrible regret in the office for having forgotten to pour the milk in the dog's bowl. I am talking of life, isn't it? And yet biographies bypass all this.

Balbir Uncle had told me about some letters you had left me. I had looked for them casually, and never found them. And then one day, as I rummaged among old rubbish, small Chinese locks for suitcases, Dad's blazer buttons, some silver coins of Zanzibar and even Kutch, I discovered a key which stood out. It had a number engraved on it. I ransacked my cupboard and found a similar key with another number, asked Nishant and he confirmed my suspicion that the keys hinted at locker number and key. The rounds to the banks started but I got no joy. Walking along Janpath one day, past the optician and the glitzy shop of lampshades, I passed the Delhi Safe Deposit Vault, tucked away in the basement and went in. I showed the keys to the lady at the main counter and she said yes, these belong to our lockers. She looked up the papers and after half an hour pulled out a paper with my mother's name and signature and with me as the co-owner of one vault. The usual identity problems, signature to be attested by the bank, proof of residence, any residence. The Pan Card had not become intrusive in those days. I went back and came with the documentation, including my marriage certificate, and they let me into the steel-barred chamber, told me how to open the lock, inserted their own key and all was hunky dory. Balbir Uncle had told me to be wary, mother couldn't have left me any money. True enough, there were two letters in your hand Mama and a thick sheaf of papers, again in your neat hand. Will have to go through these, I sighed ruefully, sorry Mama, embarrassed to say this. But I looked forward to the two letters. Yes, and there was an envelope with my name written on it in grandmother's hand in Hindi. Yes it had money, and I stood there and felt mean counting, but it was fifteen thousand and a little over. She must have saved up for me, and a small note inside which said, 'Your mother being what she is, I thought I should leave you something.' And there was a plain gold chain, nothing fancy, but gold all the same, and over seventy hundred-rupee notes. Well well. I left the money in the locker. As I came out the old lady at the counter said, 'You are not smiling!' I put on a smile, tough thing to do, for emotion had got the better of me, dealing with you and your mother, both gone. A letter or a note sprung on you from the other bank, and I am talking of river banks here, can unsettle you for a moment.

I went home, laid the sheaf of papers aside and opened the envelope marked 'Letter 1'.

My dearest Seema,
I haven't been half as good a mother as my mother was to

me. This realization has come to me quite late and such understanding is always accompanied by guilt. Women have their duties cut out, as you must have experienced. You are supposed to cook, look after husband and children and mother-in-law, press and knead her aching shins, also knead the dough for the parathas. Fortunately, we always had someone to help out, could afford it, but just about. And we have to give children to our husbands—and to ourselves. Life is incomplete without them, and the taunts, both spoken and unspoken, float around till the uterus flowers. A country becomes backward because of backward beliefs which sit on our shoulders like Baital on the shoulders of Vikramaditya. Children are an absolute duty, especially daughters, more especially after the time of blood. I did what I could, but I was already old; wasn't I close to fifty when I got you, all against medical advice and your father's misgivings? He was reconciled to be a childless parent.

My political passions, and there was a time I thought I had none other, took me away from life. If life was a river, I hardly ever crossed it—sounds a bit high-flown, a bit poetic and a bit untrue. (Anything to do with poetry has to be a bit high-flown and a bit untrue.) Words are, unknowingly, a bit treacherous, innocently treacherous; they never tell the whole truth, they can't, it's the inability of letters to cope with life.

I do not wish to give you any advice, firstly because you won't comprehend it, secondly you won't follow it, and lastly because you may laugh at it. That would hurt, were you to laugh. And yet by the time you read this I may be beyond hurts. Don't follow one particular passion at the cost of all else. It is not worth it, for all you know even love—the kind we hear of in stories, may not be worth it. Life is bigger than any one solitary passion, how repetitive can I be. Yet, I went that way and my father, Thakur Brajbir Singh, never tried to stop me, while my mother looked askance at what was going on. And life is really nothing, if not compromising at many turns. It is not a bad word, compromise, but I learnt that too late, having spurned it two-thirds of my life.

You suffered because of me and my shadow. You were told by my mother, though how I shouted at her then, that you were not as talented as I was, had not ventured into languages as I had. You gave up a bit early, but then we all have to go our way. We can't walk the roads others have marked out for us, we make our own maps, and that's how it should be.

Your father and mine have left enough for you, including the house in Qaiserbagh and the cottage in Kangra, and please see to it that they remain in your solitary name. Quite a bit has gone into your dowry, you know all that, and while I wouldn't have bothered, your grandparents as also your father are very happy that you have gone into a Thakur household and not a pen-pushing Kayastha family.

Open the second envelope when you are alone and at peace with yourself. You could be a bit surprised. I feel it is too autobiographical. But it is Letter 3 that I am concerned about. You may be in for a shock, but nothing you can't withstand. You are quite tough, you are my daughter.

With lots of love,

Shail

I waited a day, and then another, absorbed the first one, had no idea I had been 'neglected' and was not going to moan over it now. If you defer a thing once, you can defer it forever—tomorrow and tomorrow and tomorrow. In any case, old words are dead words, or aren't they?

Dearest daughter,
In the late twenties, I was in Bombay working with my siblings, meaning brother communists. I had slugged it out for two years going street by street and telling the people what imperialism meant for India, and also what the capitalist class, the factory owner and his kow-towing confidantes meant for the heroic labour and the forgotten peasant. Despite walking with workers, dressing plainly, eating *pau bhaji* from stalls just like them, they still felt I was a stranger. It was the way they glanced at me for a micro second. They looked torpid and fatigued—the news from Moscow had not been very encouraging. MN had been left out of the Comintern, I mean expelled. He had been accused falsely of being a renegade; all this after one Kuusinen attacked him at the Sixth World Congress. He distorted Roy's thesis and said Roy had made out that British imperialism would lead India to freedom. Can you imagine anything more absurd? Our Indian brethren believed whatever Moscow said. Stalin's word was law. Money also came from Moscow, never mind if their own peasantry was starving. And then, suddenly, there blew a sudden gust of breeze through the lot, I saw faces smiling away and conspiratorial whispers. I asked Patankar, a staunch communist. He was always dressed in a neat shirt and trousers and told me one day that he always wore crumpled kurta and pyjama formerly but when he turned red and looked at the congressmen dressed in that garb,white cap and dirty kurta flapping around the knees, he decided to wear neat shirt and pant, merely to distance himself from them. He told me that one Dr Mahmud had come to Bombay and set up a sort of hush hush camp, he couldn't be from anywhere but Moscow. No one knew half as much—not Dange, not Tayab Sheikh,

not Sundar Kabadi. Within a few weeks Patankar managed to get to him. 'Can I see him?' I asked Patankar. 'I'll have to ask Dr Mahmud,' he answered. But don't ever talk about him. Once the police get a sniff, he will be in the cooler.

Two weeks later, Patankar brought word that the doctor will see me. It was a small two room tenement somewhere in Kalbadevi. Dr Mahmud was sitting on a chair with a small cheap table in front, tall man with a thick scruffy beard that hadn't been trimmed for some months. There were cane benches in rows facing him, and a good dozen people sitting there and listening to him attentively. I recognized a trade union leader who waved at me and smiled. The doctor did not waste more than a glance at me. I had been careful to dress smartly in a well-starched sari. And I was wearing heels. His talk was ending and there was a lively discussion which I didn't choose to join, and then I noticed a boy dressed fairly shabbily bring in small cups of hot roadside sugary tea for all.

The third time I came to his brilliant dissertations, I ventured to speak and in a low voice. I also made it a point to speak in a very Indian accent, broadening my t's and d's. As long as you dwell on the consonants an extra second or so, no one can tell if you are desi or convent-educated, as some of us are called, or someone who has lived abroad. As we were filtering out I asked him, 'Sir I hope you are being looked after—meals and things, you know. Can I help in any way? I could cook a decent meal for you?' He thanked me for my concerns. 'Does anyone give you tea in the morning? Is it the same dirty roadside tea stall?' He nodded. I walked into the kitchen and saw a kerosene stove and some ordinary crockery. Next morning I walked in with eggs, a jug of milk, green Lipton tea, coffee powder, and brown bread. I fried eggs for him and put up a fairly decent breakfast. He seemed happy, almost child-like. I improved his crockery and things, and on the seventh, or was it the eighth visit, I asked him, 'Dr Mahmud, what do you think is happening in Mexico—after all it had the first communist party outside Russia, and possibly Germany?'

'Mexico is old hat now, and this Soviet type communism will also become old hat one day. Life moves on. But you were wrong, Germany did not have a communist party before Mexico.'

'Despite Rosa Luxemburg?'

'Despite,' he nodded.

'Dr Mahmud, don't you remember Mexico at all, the Geneva Hotel, the munitions man, Alfonzo, Ramos and that fabulous cook of yours? I forget her name. Have you had a memory loss?' He was jolted, I could see.

'I thought you looked familiar, there was something about you with a smell of the past.'

'Scent, you mean. I am Shail, your secretary.'

After a long pause he asked, 'What are you going to do now?'

'I am going to stay in Bombay for a while. But eventually I have to get back to California.'

'I didn't mean that.'

'Then what did you mean?'

'Never mind.'

'I hope you didn't think that I would shout from the housetop who you are.' I didn't say what I wanted to. I hope he wasn't asking whether I would go to the police. A storm of outrage rose within me but I stifled it. Never act on impulse, I keep telling myself. And yet, within a month, the police got to know and took him in. The next day, I took a flight out of Bombay to Singapore and then back to America before the police could hunt me out.

That was the second letter. The next day I opened the third envelope.

Dear Seema,

Before I break the news, I must say that it is time which makes us do so many things which we would not have done otherwise. The times also dictate how the world treats you. America was at war with communism, and I was at least two-thirds American, having spent over thirty years in Canada, Mexico and the States. It is going to be a shock, but I may as well get it off my chest as soon as possible. I was in jail in the US for a good four months and wouldn't have been out so soon but for my contacts with Markham who had by then retired but still wielded clout, and his camp followers. Don't worry, it wasn't felony! It's in my stars; I don't get on with famous men. The two men I am going to blame may have never heard of me, but their followers certainly did, and they were the ones who did me in. To be a member of a communist party needed a lot of courage anywhere outside the Soviet Union. America was the worst; it was saddled with Joe McCarthy and Edgar Hoover. Of the two, Joe was worse. My troubles arose in the fifties when you were two or three years old, but as far back as 1947, this rogue had said in a radio debate that he was in favour of outlawing the communists. Worse, he had also stated that 'All communist aliens should be forced to leave the country'. And he wanted people belonging to 'front organizations' to be finger printed. Some of us, and by that I mean we communists, had brought it upon ourselves.

Many of us hid the fact that we were members of the party. I never hid the fact. The FBI, under Hoover, put its nose to the ground and exposed them. It compiled a 1700 page dossier against the party. It inveigled Catholic priests like Fulton Sheen whose weekly broadcasts had made him very popular, to rail against communists. McCarthy's anti-communism was not a wave, for some time it was the sea itself.

Books won't tell you about the fear and suspicion hovering over America then. The early cold war itself was frightening and the fact that Soviet Russia had managed to test the atomic bomb cast a shadow over the entire West. On 1 October 1949 Mao Tse-Tung announced the founding of the People's Republic of China. Chiang Kai-shek had been decisively beaten. And don't forget the Korean War and the fact that three times the North Koreans crossed the Thirty-Eighth Parallel, driving the South Koreans and Americans down. To cut it short, I was interned. I am sure you can get more details from Balbir and books.

Your mother,
Shail

Balbir Uncle was more critical of communists than of McCarthy or so I thought at first. When you look at something dispassionately, your critical faculties come to the fore. He started by saying, 'I'll tell you what I felt during those years. Subconsciously, Shail had followed her mentor MN, who had forgotten his country, or I should say for whom revolution came first and India next. Let's be fair. For MN it could be attributed to intellectual arrogance during the twenties while he was hobnobbing with the commie hoi polloi in Moscow. What of Shail? That he did not even recognize her in Bombay must have been a blow. I am just guessing, Seema. She too forgot the country for a while; I have no evidence to back that up though, not a word. Instead, she plunged into communism. For a while things were looking bad for the planet but good for the Communist Party in America. Hitler had risen and the European democracies had not stood up to him. The American communists wouldn't see the difference between the Nazis and other bourgeois democracies initially, but were clever enough to change track after Munich 1938, when Chamberlain succumbed to Hitler. 'Peace in our time'—the fellow declared. Earl Browder, who led the American Communist Party, declared 'Communism is twentieth century Americanism'. Their membership doubled from a measly forty thousand to eighty in no time. Then came the Soviet Non-Aggression Pact with Germany. I remember the date: 23 August 1939. Russians were easily mollified by Stalin. It was a case of Germany versus the democracies, one bourgeois government against another. How are we revolutionary communists of the Soviets bothered? We just want peace.

But in America the commies started being looked upon as enemies or at least as proxies of enemies. Can't tell you the number of times the American communists lost it. They had bungled when their leaders spoke against the New Deal during the Depression. They lost it when they believed the trumped up, spurious confessions of Bukharin and Radek in the mid-thirties. They lost it again when the Molotov–Ribbentrop agreement was announced and Americans said these communists are breaking bread with the Nazis. You can't survive if every ill wind in Moscow makes you shudder and change your stance. And there was this master of half-truths—Joe McCarthy. When it comes to calumny, half-truths are worse than untruths. Lies are disproved, people can see through them. Half-truths are insidious. Americans believed Joe. Even 'fellow traveller' became an expletive, you could kill someone with it. When President Truman fired General McArthur, Joe McCarthy said of the president, 'The son of a bitch should be impeached'. And he kept saying 'I can investigate anyone'. He was too big to bother about Shail, but his myrmidons took care of her. Edgar Hoover of the crew cut and the regulation dark socks took her in. She never hid her membership and your parental house had shelves of secret books—including Gorky and Turgenev, don't laugh. There was a portrait of Marx, beard and paunch intact, hung in her study. I think she got four months in the cooler, though with you, two, or was it three years of age, it seemed like a year. When she came out, your dad decided to move back to India. Seema didn't argue. A few months later our dad, Thakur Brajbir Singh asked her, what she wanted, how she proposed to live her life now. Mind you, he was in his seventies. She answered, 'I just want the solace of old melodies from Indian films; and I want to look after Seema.'

❁

But I must get on with my own life. A month after the minister died, Nishant was transferred to the agricultural ministry. Within a month he was off on a tour—again abroad this time. 'So you are in with the minister of your new ministry as well?' I asked. He just shrugged his shoulders. He was hardly away for three or four days and was back.

Shambhu Nath and Ram Dollar Pande

You can't duck things in life Mama, they have a habit of catching up with you. On the political scene, there had been tectonic changes—the Morarji breakdown, the lame duck government of Charan Singh for six months, then the elections and the resurrection of Indira Gandhi. Then came the death of Sanjay Gandhi and Nishant's minister in the mines. Going into the mines was like going into the underworld for him, and there is never any return from the underworld. Rumours had started flying, who was it who sent him to inspect the mines? Who could it be? Thank God, Nishant was not with him.

But as I said, things have a habit of catching up with you. I've come to that conclusion. You carry a letter to someone unknown thinking the guy is straight and being harassed by a vindictive state. He turns out to be a wife-burner. One of the unique triumphs of our ancient Hindu culture is wife burning. Formerly we did it by putting her on the hubby's funeral pyre; now you can't wait that long, you burn her before you die. Just a switch in timing, Mama. Well, Inspector Ambika Singh saw to it that the man was hunted down and charged even if Shambhu was a staunch Jana Sanghi and his brother, Ram Dollar Pande, had financed the party. The first I knew of the case was when Bipin phoned me. Bipin Kumar, classmate of Nishant in college, had got me off the hook, remember Mama? Bipin phoned to say that Shambu Nath Pande had been charged for murder and abetment to murder, and his brother Ram Dollar Pande had hired him. Of course, he wouldn't be caught dead using a word like 'hired', a bit stuffy, this Bipin, like all lawyers. He had got the 'brief' he said, or something like that and the case was in court. 'Which one?' I asked. 'Tees Hazari,' he answered, and I let out a laugh, recalling how he had snubbed me in Lucknow.

'Why are you telling me all this, Bipin? I have nothing to do with the case.'

'Yes, but you never know about the prosecution. Ambika Singh has investigated the case, hard nut to crack.' I didn't like the drift, why was he going on about all this? I wasn't too happy when he dropped a hint that he hadn't said a word about the case to Nishant. 'I have nothing to hide from Nishant,' I lied. And I hadn't told Nishant a thing about it. Alfie, the letter and money, and the auto ride to Faizabad Road. A fortnight later I get a summons! I get a summons—defence witness in Shambu Nath Pande vs The State of India. That moment I could have killed Bipin. It was not Ambika Singh who had called me. It was Bipin, the one who disdained practising in Tees Hazari Courts, who had got me summoned. I refused to answer his phone calls. I made my quiet enquiries about the long trail leading on to Tees Hazari. Jana Sangha pressure did not cut any ice with the Home Ministry—Charan Singh, the home minister, would not budge. But they managed to put the investigation in the cooler by putting pressure on the Lucknow Police, that is until a scatter-brained DIG decided to hand over the investigation to Inspector Ambika Singh.

Ambika found a sealed envelope pertaining to the case in the Malkhana, the store room where all these articles from blood-stained daggers to country-made pistols are stored. The envelope contained the broken bangles which were found on the staircase of Shambu Nath's house. Ambika was convinced that it was murder. Ram Dollar Pande had got the case transferred to Delhi, citing strong bias of Lucknow Police and Ambika Singh. That was during the Janta regime. I always knew that time takes its own time to screw you.

I was tense, not just because I was to appear in court, but also because Nishant knew nothing of my escapade. He had got scent of the fact that I was following the case in the papers and once asked why I was interested in Shambu Nath Pande and Ram Dollar Pande. Was it the Lucknow connection? But I fobbed him off by saying I was just interested in the case, one gets hooked on murder cases at times. But half-truths get mapped across my face easily Mama, as you would know, and he noticed the map-lines, I could see it in his eyes, but never said a word.

I waited for two hours before being called up but there was no sign of the hearing. I went for chai at one of the stalls and returned just in time to hear my name called, 'Seema Singh, wife of Nishant Singh IAS, *hazir ho*.' The team setup by Dollar Pande to save his brother was furious that I was late to 'adduce' evidence as they put it, Mama, never heard the silly word earlier. I was almost panting as I took the oath while Bipin Kumar glared at me as he started the examination. It went something like this:

Bipin: 'Mrs Seema Singh, do you know Mr Alfred Hemmings, Defence Witness(DW 2)?'

(DW 1 was Shambhu's cook who had lied that Bahuji, meaning murdered wife, was never ill-treated, was the rani of the house, she even had the keys to the safe, and accidentally caught fire, ran helter-skelter, flailing her arms, hitting the walls, and hence the broken bangles.)

Seema: 'I know him, he was almost in hiding when I met him…sorry, I first met him when the police and doctors arranged a vasectomy camp in Qaiserbagh. Mr Alfred was also present.'

Bipin: 'Did some untoward incident take place that day?'

Seema: 'Every incident was untoward that day. If you are forced against your will and confined, it would surely be classed as untoward, wouldn't it?'

Judge: 'Witness will only answer. Counsel for defence will ask questions.'

Bipin: 'Do you recognize anyone else here who was present on this occasion in Qaiserbagh?'

Seema: 'I recognize Ambika Singhji, inspector.'

Bipin: 'What was the inspector doing there?'

Seema: 'He was as good as organizing the nefarious vasectomy camp.'

Judge: 'Witness will refrain from adjectives. Word "nefarious" to be expunged.'

Bipin: 'What was happening at this camp?'

Prosecutor: 'Objection.'

Bipin (interrupting): 'What did you personally see happening at the camp?'

Seema: 'I saw the police and hospital staff and even doctors forcing poor people on the street into the tents so that they could perform vasectomies. I never went into the tents, never tried either, for no one would have allowed me into the tents where the operations were being performed.'

Bipin: 'Was any police officer of higher standing than Inspector Ambika Singh present there?'

Seema: 'No, he was the senior-most cop.'

Bipin: 'Senior-most cop organizing shameful, forced sterilization camp?'

(Mayhem, Mama, the prosecutor up in arms, shouting away. Character assassination of upright police officer, and all that. Court asked Bipin to re-phrase the question.)

Bipin: 'Inspector Ambika Singh was in charge of the camp, wasn't he?'

Seema: 'From the law and order perspective, yes. There were doctors there too.'

Bipin: 'What was Mr Alfred Hemmings doing there and did you meet him later?'

Seema: 'He is a reporter and was observing the camp so that he could report on it, obviously. Yes, I met him later when he came to my house, where we had a long discussion on the Emergency—I even asked him if it would ever end.'

Prosecutor (interrupting): 'Your Honour, this has nothing to do with the case, whether the Emergency began or ended, and if it was good or bad has nothing to do with the accused burning his wife.'

Judge (ignoring): 'Continue.'

Seema: 'Thank you, Your Honour. We discussed the Emergency,

since both of us were against it, and we had dinner.' (I could have kicked myself seconds later for saying that).

Bipin: 'Did anything else transpire in the meeting?'

Seema: 'He requested me to carry a letter for a man whose hardware shop both of us had seen being sealed by Inspector Ambika Singh. He told me the owner's name was Shambu Nath and that he was being victimized since he was a member of an opposition political party. He was on the list of people to be arrested and was on the run.'

Prosecutor: 'Objection, hearsay.'

Bipin: 'Your Honour, DW 1, Mr Hemmings has already stated this. Witness is merely corroborating what he said.'

(There was a big argument after this, prosecution saying that time after time the non-existent police list is coming up for evidence, when no such list has been placed by the defence on record. Bipin stated that these were confidential lists maintained by the same police which was prosecuting the innocent defendant.)

Bipin (resuming examination): 'Why, in your opinion, did Alfred Hemmings ask you to take the letter to the defendant? Why couldn't he carry it himself?'

(They wrangled over this too, the prosecutor saying that he should have asked this off Hemmings. Judge ignored the objection.)

Seema: 'Because he had been writing very strongly against the government, and police was after him. It would have been worse for him if he had been caught with a letter to a suspect.'

Bipin: 'So you volunteered?' (I nodded, both the judge and Bipin barked simultaneously, 'Speak up.' I said, 'Yes, I acceded to his request.' Then Bipin asked, 'How did you deliver the letter?')

Seema: 'I phoned up first since I had been given a telephone number. Having ascertained the address, I went there and delivered the letter.'

Bipin: 'Did you meet Defendant Shambhu Nath Pande there?'

Seema: 'No, I never met any male. I just handed over the package, I mean the envelope, to the lady I had spoken to on the phone. She took the letter in and I left.'

Bipin: 'Did you have any inkling that the defendant was a fugitive from a crime?'

Seema: 'Not in the least. The only crime for which he was hiding was that he belonged to a political party. If I had known he was accused, however wrongly, of a crime, I would never have consented to deliver the letter. He was being harassed and his shop sealed because he was from another party.'

Bipin: 'Thank you, that will be all.'

The prosecutor now got up, thin, tall, sallow-faced, I noticed his large shoes. He addressed the court saying, 'I don't know why my learned defence counsel put the honourable witness on the stand since all she said was that she delivered a letter to the accused. Actually, he was trying to put words in the mouth of the witness and trying to lead good character evidence, which is inadmissible. So the prosecution pleads that the entire testimony of the witness be disregarded and expunged from the record.'

The judge said, 'Nothing doing, if you had objections to the line of examination, you should have approached the court then. Proceed with the cross examination.'

Prosecutor: 'Seemaji, what made you think that Shambhu Nath, the wife-murderer ('Objection!' screamed Bipin, prosecution is trying to influence witness. 'Sustained,' said the judge, 'Public prosecutor is advised to be careful.') I will rephrase the question, what made you think that Shambhu Nath was being hunted by the police? Mr Alfred Hemmings told you?'

Seema: 'Yes.' (Bipin was again up in arms, 'Objection! He is leading the witness!' This was accompanied by a theatrical imploring look at the judge which would have done credit to a thespian. I realized now why Bipin was so successful. Judge rebuked Doodnath Singh, the prosecutor.)He repeated the same question and I answered, yes, Alfie told me.

Prosecutor: 'Alfie?'

Seema: 'I mean Alfred.'

Prosecutor: 'Oh, first name terms, I see! I mean, pet name terms! So whatever he told you, this Mr Alfred Hemmings of the *Christian Science Monitor*, Alfie to you Seemaji, you poor innocent lady took as gospel truth?'

Seema: 'Come on everyone from the cobbler to the collector's aunt knew that he was on the run, every politician was in jail, none could breathe free air. Were you in India those days or some place in Casablanca?' (I heard a titter in the court room, and saw the judge smiling.)

Prosecutor: 'You would know something about free air, Seemaji. You must have drawn a deep breath as you stepped out of jail. Was it one night in jail? (Bipin had almost jumped on his chair, shouting 'Objection! Attempt to defame witness—character assassination!' The fucking Doodhnath Singh appeared astonished. 'Your Honour, this incident is a positive testimonial to the witness. She opposed the Emergency, was prepared to slap a constable and go to jail. It was in a good cause. Is it the learned counsel's opinion that opposing the Emergency takes away from her standing?' He shook his head disbelievingly, the rogue. The judge cut him short saying, 'Be careful, Mr Doodhnath Singh, but objection overruled. If witness went to jail for whatever reason, court should know. Witness will answer the question.' By now I had forgotten the ruddy question, Mama. Was thinking about what the press would make of it and how my husband would react. I sensed how darling hubby would react. I made it clear that I had forgotten the question.)

Prosecutor: 'Mrs Seema Singh, I asked you if you spent one night in jail or two?'

Seema: 'Two.'

Prosecutor: 'I have full sympathy with you and your ideals, Mrs Singh, as also the fact that you and the accused were on the same side—I mean doctrinally—you both were anti-Emergency, as any right thinking set of persons would be. But who told you that the accused belonged to the Jana Sangh? Was it Alfie again?'

Seema: 'It was, but come on, all shopkeepers are Jana Sanghis, aren't they?' (This was again followed by a titter in the court.)

Prosecutor: 'And come to think of it, aren't these party members anti-feminist also, in your opinion?'

Bipin (addressing the court): 'Your Honour, this anti-feminism which the learned prosecutor had sprung on the witness is not really germane to the issue.'

Judge: 'German? What have Germans got to do with this?'

Bipin: 'I meant it is irrelevant.'

Prosecutor: 'The learned counsel's English is rather exclusive, Your Honour. While Mr Kumar's knowledge of law is profound, I have known legal practitioners who cover up their deplorable ignorance of law with high class English.'

(The judge smiled at the witticism, Bipin bristled and the cross, as everyone calls it, resumed.)

Prosecutor: 'Did you meet Alfred after this? Sorry, you have already admitted that you met again, and you even talked about dinner, soup, chicken curry, rice pudding if I remember alright?'

This time, Bipin Kumar protested in a measured voice. 'Learned Prosecutor is turning cross-examination into vaudeville, if I have guessed alright.' A half titter, pretty restrained, went around the court room, but Mama, the judge did not know the meaning of vaudeville, so Bipin had to clarify that it meant 'lower cusp of comedy Your Honour, could pass off as nautanki in our local cultural milieu, perhaps.' Bipin seemed to be on the lower cusp of pomposity, I thought. High flown English in a syrupy accent, Latin quotes—*mens rea, ignorentia juris non excuzat*, all score high marks in law courts, Mama. That bloody Doodnath Singh was right. No wonder the Parsis seem to be doing so well in this profession, even though they are good at nothing else. And they eschew the word '*saala*' in court. They had some fighters once, now they can only fight among themselves where they do not eschew the word 'saala' and other sisterly swear words.

Judge: 'Please cut out the fat, Mr Doodnath Singh, will you?'

Prosecutor: 'Why did Mr Alfred ask you to deliver the letter? You had never acted as his messenger earlier, I am sure.'

Seema: 'I already answered that, Alfred Hemmings was being hounded by the police because of his anti-Emergency articles. If he had been caught with a letter to a fugitive, what shall I call him…'

Prosecutor (interrupting): 'Wife-burner.'

Seema: 'Politico, it would have gone badly for him.'

Prosecutor: 'And what time did he leave?'

Seema: 'Next morning.'

Prosecutor: 'Oh, so he spent the night with you…I mean… (but by then pandemonium broke in the court room—the Pandies were back in the shape of Bipin and of course, Doodnath Singh, the prosecutor—his apologies…slip of the tongue…what I actually meant…blah blah. I don't see any point in going on, Mama.)

❁

Not since the summons first darkened my door did I dream this up. It was after my forgetful foray into the court room, and the cross, as they call the cross examination, that I spent hours at night thinking about it, conjuring up visions, images—black stairway, badly lit or not lit at all except for the kerosene oil-induced fire leaping on blouse and sari. She doesn't know where to run, the face she turns to is grim and stone-hard, jawline clenched, the language between two pairs of eyes has dissolved; the hurl-and-stumble down the stairway, but the door down there where the stairs end their curved descent is bolted, you can't struggle against an iron bolt, not with fire climbing into your hair, the door could even be locked, how would she know(?) the fire has more folds, more pleats, than the sari she wears, scalp turning into a lit awning, and the last creaking climb to the landing is almost inter-stellar; and glass everywhere, it cracks with heat, doesn't it, window glass and red bangle.

I don't see much point in telling you about the fight with Nishant. I got a tongue lashing as you can expect and kept mum. Silence is best when you have no defence. But how would I or Alfie have known anything about Shambhu Nath's relations with his wife or his passion for his mistress, the Bambaiya Hindi wali? I just kept quiet. The blaze of his anger was something to be felt. Even a week later his mouth remained grim, as also his silence. Things appeared in the Delhi editions of the national papers. Fortunately there was nothing salacious about the items. Such things between husband and wife don't end with a verbal assault. With each such incident or quarrel he withdrew for a week or more at night. I would wait for his touch in vain. Is he punishing me or himself? Can I ever reach the underbrush of his perceptions? Is it the flip side of violence what he is practising, this dry icy abstemiousness? And one last horrid thought, does such an escapade of mine render him impotent?

With time such incidents normally recede into a black memory and normality returns. Normally. Sometimes they lead to other things. His sister, Giribalaji, rattled in on her old Ambassador car one afternoon when I was alone in the house. I didn't like the expression on her face, as usual unsmiling, when she met me. She wouldn't sit down. She declined my offer of a sherbet or a soft drink. 'I haven't come to sit down or chit-chat,' she said. I could have asked her then why on earth she had come, but refrained. I waited for her to go on.

The fact that I didn't utter a word may have irritated her further. You never know she may have expected me to say 'Arre bhabhi or didi, (or whatever they say in these silly old zamindari households), you seem put off, what have I, poor me, done to annoy you, revered sister-in-law?' I wouldn't be caught dead saying things like that. She came out with the first volley.

'You still don't seem to have come out of your adolescence,' she said as an opening gambit. First, pull at the peace pipe, Mama. I kept mum. 'You need some tutorials on behaviour,' that was the second volley, as she kept looking me in the eye. I didn't react or flinch or stare back angrily. But our eyes got locked—mine expressionless, hers hostile. She seemed to be looking at me through the sights of a gun. I just waited for her to go on, my face devoid of expression. Impassivity can irritate people, I was to discover.

'Good looks alone don't make a wife. You don't seem to understand! You are causing a lot of anxiety and embarrassment to my brother. We are getting a bit tired of all this.'

'We? You and your husband or you and my husband?'

'Yes, me and my brother, your husband. We thought you'd improve, but...'

'Improve?'

'Yes, improve, but you seem to be still the silly old girl that you were when he regrettably married you.' I always knew the family was against the marriage. 'Are you making a reference to his regrets or mine? Even if I had regrets I wouldn't be caught dead sharing them with anyone, not even his sister. But I have none, I mean regrets.' She was stunned.

'Wives are not supposed to even think of regrets. It is a sin.'

'Oh, so it is just the hubby's prerogative, is it, this

matrimonial legacy of regrets? I could have married Anne, why did I marry Susanne?'

There was silence for a while. I kept quiet waiting for her to go on. 'You speak out of turn, way out of turn. You are a wife, not the master in the house, understand!'

'There are no masters in this house.'

'It is good to have a master, good to have his word prevail. Obedience is a virtue, and it is not optional, obedience I mean. Do you understand? In Bihar there always is a master.'

'In UP there isn't.'

I didn't see it coming Mama, but her palm came hard on my left cheek and stayed there. You could have heard the slap sitting in the next room. It stung. All I said was, a bit menacingly, 'Don't try that again lady or you'll regret it!' She turned around and left. One is small Mama, the first thought that came to mind was 'Thank God there was no servant in the house to witness this.' And I was also relieved that her driver had not seen the incident. Cars were always parked on the side. A mean thought occurred later, could this have been planned between brother and sister? No, couldn't have ever been. I think the glum-faced *churail* decided to show initiative and come to her brother's aid. Also wondered what she would tell her brother about the episode, what spin she would put on it. And spin comes easy to some women.

I decided not to mention the visit to Nishant when he came home. One can't dissemble though and I was as glum faced as stocky, well-fleshed Giribala, my darling sister-in-law. When turmoil strikes, we women turn into archaeological sites Mama, layers of anger, depression, day-dream piled upon day-dream; Mohenjo-Daros, layer on layer of history and life in stone, left in stone. The night is an adversary, how to negotiate him, and that is not the end of it, sleeplessness and a bad dream you can make nothing of, are sure to disembark on me. And the day will be a wallow, time you have to somehow pass. Anger, humiliations and other indeterminate emotions crowded my brain. The mind can also fabricate a lot. I tried to switch off, but what if something similar were to happen again? I was damned if I was going to let that happen. Do I tell Nishant? I was looking for equilibrium which does not come easy Mama, as you would know, once you are disequilibriumed. Even if it, or a part of it, by which I mean this illusory calm descends on you, remember it has come through a forest of bramble. Well, if it must descend on my eyes or head it needs ankles, feet.

Thoughts see-sawed. When she slapped me I felt naked. Then at the end of a sterile rumination I thought, 'What's in a slap?' For a Bedouin woman slapped by a stocky elder(ly) bitch fed on camel milk, her face wrinkled leather, it would not have counted even as an ululating moment. Some minutes later my anger would rise like a gas flare. The mind is inexhaustible—it keeps thinking, if whatever traverses through it can be called thought. Let me sleep, I would tell it. Who was the guy who talked of solitary contemplation? My thoughts were like a Mongol horde, nothing solitary about them. Another thing about the mind is, it is no good at erasures, till the desertification of the mind follows and the unawareness of the moment when you slide into sleep.

Next morning, in the half-light preceding daybreak, I looked at Nishant's face, broad forehead devoid of lines, flat as a runway, face devoid of wrinkles, anxieties and thoughts of tomorrow. What are anxieties but thoughts of tomorrow? Do I know this man? Do I know this face and what goes on behind that smooth unlined forehead of his?

Will I wait for things to settle down, resolves to get worm-eaten with time? Will the hurt go? Will Nishant and I laugh at all this one fine day? The day you forget the dark chamber your thought and mood were in, you'll be free I tell myself. But this was, if I look at it as an ordinary middle class woman, an event as large as an oil rig, wasn't it Mama? I nurse my hurt, I forget comforts, I walk out on my body. Daksha came in like a blessing at noon. I served *chaach*, our buttermilk, and some snacks. She said that her five-year-old daughter returning from school the other day asked her what 'inner self' meant. 'Tell me, Seema, how do you explain that to a child? And is the teacher mad, talking about the inner self in a class of kids who can't tie their shoe laces yet?' I couldn't tell her anything, I just kept shut. Well, she may have kept shut, but I was going to speak out. Daksha you should have told her that the outer self means your top, blouse, your school uniform. The inner self means kidney, liver, heart. We both laughed. She didn't mention her son, just a year old.

A fortnight later, I told Nishant, 'I didn't know the man, this Shambhu Nath, had no idea he had burnt his wife, or may not have burnt his wife, who knows? I took a decent man's word that he was a political fugitive, and a letter had to be passed on to him from England. Alfie is a decent man, the little I know of him. I passed on the letter to the fellow. Later all this comes up, tough luck. I'll face things as they emerge. Yes, and I hated the Emergency and do not regret hating it.' He kept quiet. I walked out of the room.

I also have a right to ruminate, Mama. The universe is never still, moves from moment to moment. You can't think of metamorphosis here. If metamorphosis becomes a continual process, a conveyor belt that brings to your senses mutation, shall we say changes in a product minute to minute, it can hardly be termed 'metamorphosis'. Reality is not just skin shrivelling over bone. It gets renewed with blood coursing through capillaries and a smile returning. Reality eddies and surges like tide, Mama. Am I making any sense? Never mind. Talking of the universe, if you are looking for the heart of the matter and find it turning into something gaseous, what does one do? What does a scientist do? Mama, I am conscious of the fact that had you been around and heard me talking this kind of nonsense, you would have exploded in anger. Breakdowns and renewals oscillate, they play musical chairs. That sounds better, doesn't it? I am wading through the wet mud of thought—sorry Mama, you'd have said mud is always wet. I will stop here squelching through the mud of my ruminations. Reality and the universe (they could be the same thing, you know) keep overwriting themselves.

Our moods didn't pick up. Each day was a wax effigy of the previous one, today mirroring yesterday, also mirroring tomorrow; days dying into silence with an inaudible sigh like a toy balloon punctured. I thought of our room as a lung that breathes; sometimes as a lung that doesn't breathe. Am I playing with thoughts the way a child cups marbles in her palms and rattles them? The nights were noisy or so it seemed, till I woke up wet with silence around me. I was not used to night-sweats and visits to the loo to peel off my nighty, sometimes twice a night. Now and then, it woke up Nishant for a moment and his face puckered up into an unspoken question, with wrinkles lining the cheekbones for a moment. In the mornings I would worry about whether the damp had smeared my skin. 'You need a washing machine,' he told me in the morning over tea. It will cost the earth I told him, those days they were imported. He shrugged. The shrug was a new development in the man. The evenings were better I must confess, for the green blossoms on the Alstonia scholaris trees gave out their strong fragrance. It was heavenly just to inhale.

The washing machine came—'I got it from the custom house confiscated items which they later give out cheaply.' He didn't have to tell me that, or probably did, seeing my questioning look. One day, I saw our sideboard cluttered with little glass baubles. What are these I asked. 'Just baubles, Seema.' It was when Daksha came in one evening that I saw the look of surprise on her face.

'That's quite something,' she said with evident joy on her face. 'Lovely Swarovski,' she added, almost catching her breath. I had not heard the word earlier and tried hard not to show my ignorance. She admired the pieces rather lovingly. Then she sat down and started talking about her son. He was over a year old and had not spoken as yet. She spilled his food on the boy and he said 'tupid', first words, and how thrilled Daksha was! Son's first words to the mom. She had come to tell me this. Our house was looking better, so was the fridge—he had brought caviar from his trip abroad. I never asked him about it. At a birthday party for him a colleague said, 'You seem to be doing well, Nishant, in the new ministry. Any travels in the offing?'

He just smiled and answered, 'The wind doesn't have a home.' He had a way with words. A few days later he said casually that we are getting a new car, well it's not new, but... and he shrugged. I was getting a bit tired of his bouncing shoulders.

'Why are we getting a new car which is not new? Our Fiat is not doing badly.'

'It is six years old,' he said. 'The car is not new, because Dad is gifting it to me. Their fortieth anniversary is just a few months off, as you know.' I didn't bloody know, didn't want to know. A few days later, a chauffeur in livery turned up with a Bavarian Motor Works car, 1980 model, a white sedan. There were a few dents, mostly on the rear fender, a scratch or two near the wheel. It didn't look old, in fact I thought it looked pretty new. 'This is a BMW, Seema. It will look new even after twenty years.' Friends smiled and clapped when they saw it. I saw to it there was no change in my looks, no sly smile, no triumphal gleam in my eye. Daksha even brought her daughter Roopali to show her the BMW. The kid was excited. Daksha looked at me quizzically, 'You don't seem to be thrilled?' It was my turn to shrug my shoulders.

There had been talk for the last month about the fortieth wedding anniversary of his parents. I didn't see much point in celebrating how the two of them had made each other miserable for four decades. His father was the archetype Thakur: domineering, dominating as males should be, isn't it, pure unadulterated *shudh* MCP. Mother-in-law mumbled and grumbled but not within his hearing, if she could avoid it. Anyway, his ear drums were getting worn out and not very keen to catch the words of others. I told Nishant that I had no intention of going, as his sister and I did not see eye to eye. He had never asked me to elaborate on the subject, but never avoided eye contact either.

It was over a month since my evidence at the Shambho Nath case. Nishant was to go alone to Bhagalpur, that's where his parents had their 'zamindari'. I had been there once and saw a servant put on father-in-law's shoes. A week before the great event sister-in-law got a severe attack of jaundice and had to be admitted in Gangaram Hospital. Now there was no excuse for me to avoid Bhagalpur, so I went, attended a party for three hundred guests, none of whom I knew. Parents-in-law came in a chariot pulled by four horses, all very feudal and faux rococo. I stayed some days there but it was depressing—the décor in the house was beige, even the tiles in the loo were brown. There were medicine chests galore—as usual, I exaggerate Mama—but there were two of them. Ma-in-law believed in homeopathy and hence one chest was full of those sugary capsules. She lived a sort of herbal life—tulsi, the desi version of basil, ginger and peppermint were her supports. And, of course, four different brands of stringent chooran to propel disturbing gases to an exit gate and the great outdoors. Cibizol and other ointments filled up father's medicine chest. After this we were supposed to go to Patna, Patliputra, if you please, hubby and I, we who were hardly exchanging say thirty words a day. Then he got a call from the ministry. Take the next train and rush back. There was no airport in that sleepy hollow called Bhagalpur. I wasn't going to miss Patna, wished to go to Bodh Gaya, had never been there before. So I went to Patna, leaving my in-laws a bit shocked and shaking their hoary heads, but never saying a word to me. We 'modern' (it's a dirty word in their lexicon) *chokris* can frighten the in-laws, that closed room, that antique bookshop called the *sasural* with its dress code—bare feet and sari *pallu*-on-head, and ritual feet touching—I believed in just folding my hands, never touched feet or knees, none of that nonsense.I did have some misgivings though, despite the *haveli* and the grain and ghee coming from the share croppers. How could the old man afford a BMW? Their own car was an Ambassador, our Birla version of the Morris Minor patronized so assiduously by our Mrs Gandhi.

I also smiled to myself about a story I had heard of father-in law. Apparently he had tried to flatter a British collector newly arrived. He told him, '*Aapne to char chand laga diye.*' When the collector asked him to translate, he said, 'You have nailed four moons on the sky.' 'Really?' said the collector, stepping out of the veranda, 'Show me.'

It was nice to get out and be on my own. Breathing easy makes you feel almost rejuvenated. Bodh Gaya was an unhappy experience. The roads were awful, single lane roads, narrow and pot-holed. A goatherd wouldn't get his flock off the road and let us pass. Almost halted us for ten minutes till after stepping on the horn for a few loud minutes we managed to bypass them. There were no books in Bodh Gaya to enlighten poor me about how Lord Buddha got his enlightenment here. Why weren't books on display? Returned late at night to Patna, had to bang on the hotel door and ring the bell a dozen times before it was answered by a sticky-eyed porter, who reluctantly let me in.

I still had two days left for my return. Train reservations are not to be tinkered with. Time can hang heavy in a hotel. Why couldn't I go and call on his former minister Budhiraja's widow? Her name was Chhaya, I remembered. I made enquiries and got hold of her address somehow through the hotel manager, who had to ring up a few people before he was successful. I took an auto-rickshaw and went across at least two hours before dusk. No phone call, no appointment. I had taken care to wear a simple sari and refrain from any makeup. As we were entering an old alley I asked the auto driver whether he had brought me to the right place. This couldn't be right. I made him stop. A country band came across the lane, carrying unlit gaslights, drums and clarinets all soundless in their hands, and a horse without a rider, awaiting the arrival of the groom. The auto driver said, 'Dalit *baraat*, madam.' I spotted some urchins at the tail end of the band and asked them about Shri Budhiraja's house. Yes, it was another furlong or so away. The auto driver took me there and I paid off the fellow. Thankfully, the house was not situated in the gullet of the lane for the lane had opened up into a small *maidan*.

I circled around the dilapidated four foot wall, broken in places, the grass inside a bit overgrown. Could this really be Chhayaji's house? Her husband was reported to have made tons of money. I opened the wicket gate and walked in, pressed the bell, which I thought never rang. I waited, did not ring again, and a maid came out and asked what my business was—very politely, of course. I gave my name. She went in and came back and asked where I had come from. I said I have come from Delhi and am the wife of Nishant Singh, once Budhirajaji's secretary. I waited—must be a good ten minutes, seated on a reed chair in the veranda, wondering when I would be asked inside. I wasn't. Chhayaji came out and stood there examining me from head to toe just as Alfie and Ambika Singh had done that morning in Qaiserbagh. I, of course, had stood up and folded my hands in a respectful namaste. She just lowered her head an inch in an almost non-existent nod. 'How did you come here?' She asked.

I told her I came in an auto and had paid the fellow off. 'That is not what I asked,' she said. I thought she meant what brought me here, and I spent half a minute on the fortieth wedding anniversary in Bhagalpur, and then my trip to Patna. Again she said, 'That is not what I asked. I wanted to know how the thought occurred to you to come and see me?' I didn't know how to answer that one. She was still standing, her face expressionless. Obviously I couldn't sit down either. Why the hell did I come here, I must have been a fool, I wondered.

'I am surprised you came. You are now big people, rich people.'

Where did that come from? I told her, the satire was misplaced and we always looked upon her as an elder, a respected elder.

'Elders can be swindled, especially in Delhi. I know of a young couple who have shifted their parents in what they call the *barsati*, the makeshift room above the garage. For the young the elders are like an old Fiat or worse, an old scooter. Actually the garage is the right place, Mobil oil on the floor, greasy dusters lying about and unwanted things, trekking boots, cricket boots a hot water bag you may need next winter. And elders aren't even needed in winter, hot water bags are more useful. Wouldn't you agree?'

I could have taken that from Nishant's or my parents. Respite came in the form of the bedraggled bandsmen we had met, suddenly coming to life and unloading their sound and fury on an unsuspecting world. She said, 'Dalits also must have *band-baja* for a wedding. Why not?' I nodded.

Where was all this leading to? I still carried the impression that she was hurt because of the fact that Nishant had not kept in touch with the family. I apologized on that score. Her reply was startling.

'He could not have remained in touch. He would not have dared.'

'Dared?' I said, angered at last, and my eyes must have shot a bit of fire. 'Why not? *Aisi bhi kya baat thi*?'

'You are very innocent,' she said after looking me in the eye for a moment. 'Have you no idea what he has done?'

I shook my head and by now I was getting nervous.

'He took away all my husband's money.' She said that emphatically and kept looking me in the eye.

'What!'

'Haven't you realized this, even if he never told you, which I naturally doubt? Your IAS colleagues tell me that he has got himself a German car.'

'He took a loan from a bank!' I said, and I'll always kick myself for telling such a blatant lie.

'Loan!' she laughed. 'How many officers take loans like that, and how many banks grant such loans for purchasing foreign cars?'

'Sorry, the loan was for a flat. The car is an old one and was gifted by his father.'

She laughed again. 'Thakur Sahib sends his *lathels*, the *lathi*-wielding retainers to get money from share croppers. Have you any idea what a BMW, even an old one, will cost, and the custom duties? You are very innocent or are you dissembling? Truly you have no idea what happened?'

I just stood there like a rock, couldn't even shake my head in denial.

'Yes, when the forty-day-ritual had passed, I took a flight to Zurich. My sister accompanied me. And when I introduced myself to the bank and showed my passport, they said that yes, he had an account but that had been closed. I asked, or rather my sister who can speak good English asked, 'How come? If an account holder dies, does the money revert to the state? Is that the Swiss law?' And the bank people said, 'No, of course not. The minister's secretary came with the right password and cleared the locker. There was not a dollar left. He had come with the minister earlier and we knew him. Even when the minister was alive, he operated the account. He paid for the locker hire charges and we closed the account.'

'When my sister persisted in questioning them they said he had taken the money in two large brief cases. We came back empty handed.' She gestured with her hands.

I stood there stupefied. She noticed the shock on my face. She repeated, you are very innocent (*Tum bahut bholi ho*). People in the IAS know all about this, there is much talk (*Bahut charcha hai iski*). This kind of talk is over a cup of chai or a glass of rum. Then people get into their cars and drive away. We remain empty handed. Another thing, this talk is in Patna. Delhi has moved ahead.

The Rustle of the Past

Breathe slow, I tell myself as I enter my room in the hotel. A waiter comes to say that dinner is served in the dining room. I thank him and ask him not to disturb me. Breathe slow, I tell myself and breathe deep. I want to be alone with sounds of the past, the rustle of the past.

What's to be done? This is what is known as shock, isn't it? Something sprung on you, and the sad part is you recognize the soil it has jumped from. You sit beside your past, or in our case, your husband's past, which coils around you and leaves its rope-burn for a lifetime. Why should his past be mine? Why must I be burdened? You steal money from someone who had himself stolen from the tax payer—theft from a thief. Even if he had got the dollars from a foreign firm, it was at the country's expense. But why am I thinking of Budhiraja? Thought should follow a straight line, should not get diverted like a river in a tangle at the estuary. The trouble is I can reach back to this past, feel it, touch it—it is no longer his alone. I have been a part of it—Zurich and Swiss Air and boarding pass, he brought me the Mallorca Pearls, remember, sold on the plane, can picture an eager arm, Nishant's arm reaching for it, air hostess smiling compassionately perhaps, as she bills him and counts the franks. I can't get around this easily.

I belong to these frayed years, I am there,clinging to one of its tassels.

How do I go on? You move against the current. But this current has already smeared you, not just skin but also entrails. I can imagine people sneering at me and him. Won't do. No salmon can fling itself against this kind of a current.

The future is a door ajar—to light or murk, I wouldn't know. I have to decide, must I always shuffle my life between him and me? Always, till death do us part?

The Quiet of the Future

The divorce took a long time.

You can marry in an hour, with or without fire as your witness, but separation is long drawn, like joined twins being carved apart. And separation does not need *agni* as *saakshi*. I don't think there were divorce courts during Vedic times. And only Gods could arbitrate between hubby and wife, Indra most likely, 'giver of barley, giver of horses', says the hymn. Shakuntala could surely have taken that forgetful king to court. Fellow must be having a favourite concubine, someone with a lot of nakhra, what's the English word for it, coquettishness? How come these English words can never do justice? Incidentally, can there be a court of law for amnesia? Suppose the court crier shouts a name and the litigant doesn't remember he is Dushyant, leave alone wife or ring?

But to business, Mama; I had moved out of the house of course, first to Daksha's, then a women's hostel in the Safdarjung Enclave. Also went to Lucknow and stayed there after the first two months of living in the Women's Hostel. By then most of the paper work was done. Mama, this would be distasteful to you and I think you are always around. So I am not going to move into a deadpan documentary of the days. I confronted Nishant, he was appalled and furious that

I had gone and seen Chhayaji without his permission, if you please, he immediately apologized for the slip of the tongue. I made it plain to him—we couldn't live together anymore.

Yes, I needed a lawyer, was damned if I was going to Bipin Babu. Daksha's husband knew lawyers—he was a property dealer—the 'realtor' word was not in vogue then. I also rang up Nigam, my editor boss in Lucknow. 'Do you know a lawyer in Delhi?' 'Why do you need one?' he asked. 'I need one,' I replied. 'Bhatnagar,' he said. Had to be a Kayasth, I said to myself. Went and met him—short man, bald except for a skimpy thatch of hair that unconvincingly hid his mustard-oiled scalp. No hair and no airs—no lofty 'I practice only in the High Court, madam.' He warned me though—you will be on the other side of life from now on, head shaking, brow wrinkling. How many sides does life have, Mama? He saw the paperwork through and the court. I did the blackmailing.

Nishant didn't want a divorce, still loved me perhaps, a bit poignant, no, who knows? I told him if you don't give in I am mad enough to expose you, and he believed me, the madness bit, I mean. Imagine the scandal I said, theft from a thief's account, corrupt minister would mean corrupt government. The Indian press would splash '*choron ka chor*'. Even stocky sister with the heavy arm and the ready palm was made to phone me up. There's nothing that can't be papered over, she said. There was also a sentence in that monologue on 'bad name', *badnami* to the family, zamindari mores, forget any slights in the past. (Slight? Sister-in-law, it was a bit heavy on my cheek.) What will you get out of it, sister! It will be a calamity for both of you. It won't be for me, I said. And he can always get another wife, I won't object, someone who can give him children. I dropped the phone, for she was in no mood to end the talk. What will my in-laws say to their neighbours in Bhagalpur? Be assured Mama, there is no wrench. And regret hasn't ever played its soft drumbeat in the night.

Flipping through life and solitude, couldn't they be the same thing? I am looking forward to it. I throw open the windows, air the house and sweep the floors. The water carrier, Mashq Mian brings in a labourer to help. He will be informing Fauzia, but I ask him to go slow, wish to be alone for a while. Hope the electricity vanishes tonight, some transformer blows up somewhere. Then I could burn an oil lamp. Wick and oil and match, and the faint glow such lamps give would be ideal for my mood. Doesn't happen, the cussed lights stay unwaveringly bright, though the street lamps are hazed with the autumn cold. All melancholy, present and past, including the one which gets housed in dreams, is being exiled from the house. Smile, look out for dawn.

So here it is, the almond tree blocking the neighbour's garden as always, a sunburnt leaf or two dropping unnoticed from its shoulders, the green canopy unwavering and loyal to the tree and to those who drink in its sight, and that includes the windows of my room, and the cool autumnal air that swirls around in the morning. My first acquaintance with a nonintrusive existence—no worries about what he will say, or what some shadow deputising for the in-laws would come out with. No brassy talk from hubby's boss. Just me to deal with, and while I know that I am a handful, I can manage. No plans, no travels, no Banaras or Badrinath, Corbett Park or Kausani. Just hang on here, grounded, don't even think of a book, not just yet. No household staff, Fauzia and her daughter could wait. A thought had occurred last evening that I should yank away the telephone line for a while, just tear it out, much in the manner one pulls out weeds. It was more an impulse than a thought, will now have time to differentiate between the two. Then I inhaled something; a vine of jasmine that had undressed and pealed a perfume from its nude waist and thrown it my way.

Qaiserbagh

Sharad Purnima, the harvest moon in October, in its bloated glory is here. For me nature's cycles seem to have resumed—harvest, threshing, cane-loaded bullock carts moving to the sugar mills, rice moving to the mandis. Good to be alone again in a smaller city, and not looking over the shoulder all the time, and worried over whether one has displeased someone! I am at peace. I don't rummage for embers in the still-warm ash of the past. Your outlook, as everyone knows, is what you make of it, every silly parent tells that to their far brighter kid. I call it the personal penumbra one carries around one. Mine is fine Mama, am looking ahead, don't worry about me. You once said to me I turn on my own axis. So did you Mama, MN and then McCarthy and Hoover. Did you ever notice, Mama, a ruthless communism attracted ruthless enemies? I think it is just time that turns on its own inscrutable axis, and our fate turns with it.

Things, of course, had happened in Lucknow. Alfie had got married to Shilpa and they had moved to England. 'That is till Mrs G comes back to power,' Shilpa had joked. Rabia had successfully resisted all the advances of the decadent Avadh nobility, sherwani-wearing, sepia drooling, tobacco-chewing gentry—and a pellet or two of opium slipped into the betel cone never did anyone any harm; their speech restricted to '*ama yaar*' while speaking to the *hum pyala*s, meaning companions of the goblet, and '*abhay murgi-ke, haram ki aulad*' while addressing the menials. Rabia married a lecturer at the university, Saleem. The family was unhappy, he came from ordinary stock. She countered by saying he was a Syed, what more did they want?

Rabia came by. My 'garden', if you could call that scabbed bit of grass fringed by a gap-toothed hedge of hibiscus, a garden, was flowerless. Neglect had deflowered it. When you are divorcing, you are not focussed on hibiscus or the almond tree. Rabia's mian had not accompanied her because he had gone to a sort of stag party. 'That means he will have a drink with them,' said Rabia with a half-smile, drinking at home would be sacrilege, taboos driven into your head remain, like a door leading to the basement which has been locked up for years. I told her she was sounding like a lecturer herself.

'I haven't made a mess of my life like you, Seema. You are drifting like a boat whose engine has stalled. I am not sure who has torn your sail. (She was mixing up her metaphors, I noticed.) What are you going to do now?' This was hardly Rabia, she had never been that direct.

'I am not looking for another sail, Rabia. I am done, and I haven't made a mess of my life as you suggest. Please remember I still have my job and there's that Pahari art book from Kangra to be completed.' She looked incredulous, hearing me.

'But what made you agree to all this?'

'To what?'

'To the divorce Seema, what else, couldn't you get around it?' Hmm, so she was thinking that hubby had shoved me out of the house. That's what people will think in Aminabad and Qaiserbagh, as they chew on their parathas and seekh kababs. It took me half an hour to explain things, and I had to avoid, rather circumvent, Zurich. You can't get Banque Suisse into a dialogue like this. A big taboo there, that was the arrangement with Nishant. Complete silence, as far as the Alps were concerned. And Giribalaji, sweet sister-in-law, had made it clear that a defamation suit would follow once the skiing on financial slopes came out in public. Divorces are not for free, *behen*. Friends can be persistent. 'Have you got a good deal out of it?' asked Rabia. 'Deal?' 'Yes damn it, I am talking alimony.' I noticed she was getting exasperated. 'How much have you got?' I thought this would not have happened in Delhi. You don't ask people about the alimony sum. Yet, if roles were reversed I would have asked her as well—small town friendships are very close. 'Half his provident fund for lifetime.'

'Is that all?' I saw shock on her face. I couldn't possibly tell her that I'd told Nishant that I wouldn't touch his Zurich dollars. 'But that's all I have,' he had said. The judge had made him part with half his bank balance. Fortunately for me, when the conversation was teetering on 'deals' and I was getting a bit edgy, Elham came in with some sherbet for Rabia, almost startling her. Elham had become a woman now, though still unmarried because of the djinn within her, after all that's what the community believed. But she hadn't done badly in studies. She could slip into a primary school either as an Urdu or a Hindi teacher. Rabia started to say something to me in startled English. 'Have you taken her in again?' I stopped her from going on any further for Elham was now well-versed in English. This little interlude did not prevent Rabia from giving me another of her wide-eyed looks. Not my day, I thought ruefully. When Elham had gone in back to the kitchen, I wanted to open out but Rabia was on an edge. 'You know, Seema, what has been happening, don't you? This girl is dangerous, she's saying all kinds of things—you've heard of them, haven't you?'

I told her I knew, she had said that Mrs G would die before the year ends. Word had got around through Mashk Mian types and stable boys and cooks to their masters as to what this girl was saying. A dire prophecy is a bomb, especially for the one who dreamed it up, and for the target if he or she gets to know of it. I knew what Elham had blurted out, and Rabia couldn't believe that I still kept her in the house.

'Rabia, I don't trust her mother who will throw her into the arms of some useless fellow. The fellow will beat her when she gets her fits or dreams or hallucinations, call them what you like. Such girls are not to be abandoned. Just because she has moved out of line doesn't mean she gets thrown to the dogs.'

That seemed to have snuffed out Rabia's disagreements with me. Tea had come in and we sat quietly sipping it.

'You think of aunty?'

'Yes, I think of mother,' (understatement of a lifetime), 'am writing to her regularly.' Rabia was not as silly as Dr Bajpai, who was scandalized when I had said something similar to her. She smiled and shook her head, 'I never know when you are joking. You will have your memories to play with now, hope they pollinate your flowers.' She hadn't said anything half as cruel to me in a lifetime. Then she added, 'I look around the landscape of your life, Seema, and find…' She stopped.

'What do you find looking at "the landscape" of my life, as you put it, dear Rabia?' Did she notice the sarcasm, for I had been stung by what she had said earlier?

'I find that you are retiring,' she said with some vehemence, and I saw her eyes watering, and gave her a hug. Water in the eyes will always get a friend a hug. 'Retiring at your age Seema, you are hardly in your mid-thirties, do you realize what it means? Retirees indulge in their addictions, gardening, orchids, an attempt at ceramics and producing uneven plates you would hesitate giving food to your dog in. Retirement means morning walks, and for the Lucknow-types, kite-flying and even quail fighting. My brother can take you to a quail fight and show you the betting, with a constable standing there and grinning away, and not charging a rupee. Yes, Lucknow can still bring a surprise out of a hat.'

'Rabia, this country has too many of them, too many people with too many addictions. Isn't Holi an addiction? We still plaster people's faces with mud, sometimes with oil paint—in honour of what? The numbers are a nightmare, people, races, religions, languages, castes, folk voices, classical voices, even the silences are too many, women's silence, hunger's silence, the silence of the casting couch. How can this mix be run by one person? No addictions for me.'

'What are you going to do?'

'I will write, Rabia.'

'I know, people scratch their shins, thighs, privates, writers do their scratching with words.'

That was most elevating. She had never been like that before. Is this an after-marriage development? Husband and sex and you open up.

Just then I got a call—a jeweller of all people wanted to chat with me. I waited for the crackle on the line to settle down and then asked him to repeat what he had said. He talked rapid fire as earlier, jasper, opal, water opal and such stones. 'These are semi-precious Madam, even divorcees can buy.' That he should have collected my personal details and phoned me up after dark enraged me, in Lucknow you didn't phone up ladies after dark, but I did not let my anger show. I told him divorcees can even buy diamonds, yellow sapphires from Sri Lanka. 'Ever heard of alimony, Jhaveriji?' He just laughed. I put the phone down. I related the phone conversation with the unknown jeweller to Rabia, even as she got up to leave. She gave me a look which spoke volumes—see what a divorce brings to your door? We hugged and she left.

In bad times politics is atmosphere, the air you breathe. Since June it had been earthquake weather. Terror was in the air, both terror and counter-terror. The clash between the Indian state and Bhindranwale, the Sikh religio-militant upstart had ended, as anyone could have forecast, with a victory for the state, a mutilated win that left the so-called victors themselves depressed and mortified. The Akal Takht, where the militant Jarnail Singh Bhindranwale had taken abode, had been brought down by the tanks. The army seldom believes in half measures. There were rumours that President Zail Singh had threatened to resign. A hundred or more Sikh soldiers from all over the country stole weapons from the armouries and proceeded towards Delhi to take revenge. People thought that Blue Star had lanced a boil. But a hundred boils sprang up after the event. And when Mrs Gandhi was shot on 31st October, just a few days after Sharad Purnima, the roof came down.

The people, meaning us Hindus, were out for blood. Sikhs were few in Lucknow, in UP as a whole, apart from a district or two in the wetlands, Pilibhit, Lakhimpur Kheri. I spent the day phoning up Daksha to ask what was happening in Delhi. Then I started getting calls from friends that I was in danger because of Elham. To hell with it, I said and laughed it off. Rabia came with her brother and Saleem, her hubby. Wasn't I glad to see him? So instinct had told them that I would shortly be in trouble.

The crowd followed, barely an hour later, licking the blood on its lips. Am exaggerating Mama, blood was what they wanted, they hadn't had much of it and were feeling sorry for themselves. Poor guys, no Sikhs, so what do you do? Buses were off road or you could always vent your anger burning the wretched things, but invariably after asking the passengers to 'de-bus' (remember Mama)—that's what our crowds today understand by Gandhism. I have always believed that people like St Francis of Assisi and our own Bapu, leave their mark on the collective soul of the people. Protests and burning buses are now synonymous. It is a sight for sore eyes, an angry crowd with a petrol can, and a police posse, stony-eyed getting down from a blue bus at the other end of the street. A bit filmy, though. Bollywood, when are you gonna leave us alone?

It was very tense, even before the crowd had uttered a word, I was sweating down my armpits. Many in the crowd were students. Slogan chanting started 'Indira Gandhi amar rahen'. 'Khoon ka badla khoon.' Then the cries for Elham went up: 'We want that woman!'

'Which woman?'

'Come on, you know all about it.'

First, we lied. We don't know who you are looking for but there's no one here.

We will then search the house, they said. They had broken the gate by now—we had obviously locked it. They rushed in and our rickety wall of Fauzia and Mashk Mian and the relatives of the gardener and the Rabia family, not the kind of phalanx that would deter a cow from entering the house, could hardly stand up against this assault. Stones were hurled at my windows and I heard the splintering of glass, which can be unnerving.Fortunately, I saw Ambika Singh stealing in with half a dozen policemen. But, he just stood. Moreover, Ambika Singh was red rag to the stud bovines among the crowd.They jeered at him and cracked filthy jokes.They now broke through and went into the rooms. Surprisingly, they did not ransack the place.They didn't find her and came out and started shouting vociferously that they would burn the house.We heard shouts for 'mitti ka thail', meaning kerosene oil. Now Ambika came forward and remonstrated. 'You can get away with anything you like today. But there will be an enquiry and you will have to pay for it.'

I lost my shit. I went in and brought Elham out. She had been locked in the storeroom. I started shouting at the crowd. 'Here she is, Elham, who I treat as a daughter.What do you want to do with her? She has not killed Mrs Gandhi. She has dreams. If she was a Brahmin, you would have said, the *devta* gets into her. But she is Muslim. Is that a crime? Tell me is it a crime to be a Christian or a Muslim at such an hour?' Just then Saleem recognized one of his students, Nirupam Khera's saala, wife's brother, a student leader in his own right. Between him and Ambika Singh they managed to get the crowd around. Ambika Singh kept shouting that I was a diehard supporter of Mrs G.We promised to light candles for Mrs Gandhi, shouted slogans for her.They left.

Rabia said, 'I will sleep over tonight. You can't be left alone.' After dinner we started talking to Elham in the living room. Two window panes had been broken and the breeze came in. I felt cold and asked Elham to get me my shawl. Elham brought it and sat on the carpet and said, 'You have had to bear a lot because of me, there was no need.' We told her there was a need, that she was blessed with a gift and that she needn't feel obliged. We were always going to defend her.

'I wish I wouldn't dream. I wish I wouldn't hear.'

Rabia asked, 'When does the dream come to you Elham?' After much goading she said, 'Mostly before first light. It is not a dream, *khwab*, it is a voice and I hear it clearly, but still as I shake myself from sleep, I start doubting whether I heard it or dreamed it up.'

I asked, 'Do you shiver or sweat when you hear the voice?' She shook her head, but then said, 'Sometimes.' Rabia then told her forcefully not to dream. 'How canI avoid it?' Elham asked. 'Even if you hear the voice, don't talk about it, if you dream of it, don't tell the world what you saw in the dream.'

'I don't see, very often I just feel.'

'Then don't feel, damn it,' said Rabia, now on the verge of exasperation. I added, 'Otherwise you will become a fake fortune-teller one day. People will come to you and you won't know what to tell them, and you will deceive yourself and them. Your life will turn into a lie.'

Rabia added, 'If you dream something bad is going to happen, and it does come about, you will put yourself in danger. And us, of course, I mean Seemaji.'

As Elham got up I asked, 'Hope you haven't dreamt of anything else?' She just stood there and didn't answer. Rabia and I sat down and said 'Tell us.' Elham looked down and wouldn't speak. After many requests she opened up. 'I have never said a word about this to anyone, have learnt my lesson. [She touched her earlobes] Do you really want to know?' And for once she smiled.

'Yes, damn it, we want to know.'

'A huge man riding on a wild donkey, with a *barcha* in his hand, a barcha with three spearheads, with lots of followers also on wild asses, will be riding towards Delhi.'

We laughed and laughed and Elham joined in, giggling away.